PARENTING TEENS
FOR A LIFE OF FAITH

BRF

15 The Chambers, Vineyard
Abingdon OX14 3FE
brf.org.uk

Bible Reading Fellowship (BRF) is a charity (233280)
and company limited by guarantee (301324),
registered in England and Wales

ISBN 978 1 80039 163 5
First published 2022
10 9 8 7 6 5 4 3 2 1 0
All rights reserved

Text by Rachel Turner 2022
This edition © Bible Reading Fellowship 2022

Acknowledgements

Unless otherwise stated, scripture quotations are taken from the Holy Bible, New
Living Translation, copyright © 1996, 2004, 2015 by Tyndale House Foundation.
Used by permission of Tyndale House Publishers, Inc., Carol Stream, Illinois 60188.
All rights reserved. Scripture quotations marked with the following abbreviations
are taken from the version shown. CEV: the Contemporary English Version. New
Testament © American Bible Society 1991, 1992, 1995. Old Testament © American
Bible Society 1995. Anglicisations © British & Foreign Bible Society 1996. Used by
permission. NCV: the New Century Version®. Copyright © 2005 by Thomas Nelson.
Used by permission. All rights reserved. NIV: The Holy Bible, New International
Version (Anglicised edition) copyright © 1979, 1984, 2011 by Biblica. Used by
permission of Hodder & Stoughton Publishers, a Hachette UK company. All
rights reserved. 'NIV' is a registered trademark of Biblica. UK trademark number
1448790. NRSV: The New Revised Standard Version of the Bible, Anglicised
edition, copyright © 1989, 1995 by the Division of Christian Education of the
National Council of the Churches of Christ in the United States of America. Used by
permission. All rights reserved.

A catalogue record for this book is available from the British Library

Printed and bound by CPI Group (UK) Ltd, Croydon CR0 4YY

PARENTING TEENS
FOR A LIFE OF FAITH

HELPING TEENS MEET AND KNOW GOD

Rachel Turner

BRF

For all the parents of teens
who graciously shared with me
their stories of pain, humour and joy.

Thank you.

CONTENTS

ACKNOWLEDGEMENTS

My husband, Mark, and son, Caleb: thank you for always believing in the book, more than I did at times. Thank you for cajoling me to get back to work, promising to play when I finished a chapter and keeping me encouraged with games and prayer. Every book I write really is ours.

My mother, Susan Hart: no matter how much I try, I will never be as wise or as generous as you are. Thank you for letting me selfishly benefit from the brilliance of you. I am so grateful to be your daughter.

My father, Terry Hart: thank you for making my teen life full of such happiness, love and adventure. I love you.

Becky Sedgwick, Anna Hawken, Kate Irvine and Iona Gray: you joined me in the pioneering adventure of piloting this material. Thank you for your relentless belief in this project, your honesty and sharpening of the material, and the overwhelming grace and love you gave me every step of the way. As with all things, this book is only complete because of your partnership.

To the rest of the BRF team: thank you for your dedication and passion.

To all my friends who keep encouraging me even though you have heard all of my book wobbles over and over again, I love you: Ell and Jo Ireton, James and Susie Yeates, Elle Bird, Elaine Sims and my Forge group.

INTRODUCTION

'I just don't know what to do anymore.' Sarah's face twisted in frustration and exhaustion as she shared her heart with me. Like many mums, she desperately longed for her son to enjoy church and have some sort of input about God. Lately, they had been heatedly clashing about his desire to play football on a Sunday instead of attending church. 'He's eleven years old, and I still don't know if God is real to him at all.' She sighed deeply. 'I don't even know if he's really a Christian. What did I do wrong?'

Agu was encouraged as his 14-year-old daughter began to talk about her faith in God. In the past she had always avoided the topic, but recently she started opening up, occasionally mentioning how she sometimes prayed at school and had conversations about God with her friends. Agu wanted to help his daughter grow in her faith, but he was unsure how to do it. He worried about getting too keen and squashing her exploration of faith. He remembered how his own parents had forced Christianity on him when he was a teenager, and he didn't want to replicate that experience with his daughter. Finding the right steps forward felt hard.

Johannes and Liz were keen that their three teenagers attend their church's youth group events. They felt that their teens didn't care about their opinions anymore, much less their faith, so the best thing they could do for their children was to get them involved in the youth ministry. One of their sons really struggled with confidence, and no matter how much they affirmed him and tried to talk with the youth leaders about him, they could feel their son shrinking more and more into himself. They knew their son had some level of relationship with God, but their hearts ached, wishing he could find the same peace, vibrancy, identity and power that they had found through their own faith and relationship with God.

From the moment our children enter our lives, our hearts begin to dream for them. We have hopes for their futures and a profound sense of wanting them to flourish in every area of their lives right now. As they grow into teenagers, we agonise over their friendships, character, happiness and self-confidence. We want the best for them. As Christian parents, our dreams for our children also include their spiritual lives. We want our children to find their own journey of faith and know the significant benefits it brings.

Our hearts are stirred up when we watch our children at church or as they head out to school, and we are filled with a desire for them to know God in a way that gives them life, makes them feel loved, helps them understand who they are and gives them a purpose on this earth.

It doesn't seem to matter whether we are single, divorced or married; whether we are new to the faith or have been raised in it; whether we have tweenagers, teenagers or grown-up children – we want more for our children spiritually than what they already have. We want all that God has for them, now and in the future.

Helping our children on their journey of faith is intended to be one of the most joyful, natural, significant parts of parenting, even when we are parenting teenagers. God designed it to be light, to be easy and to work in the chaos and beautiful mess of family life. This book won't help you conquer the entirety of parenting. I'm sorry. It would be nice if it did, but I'm not that smart. It won't teach you how to discipline a 16-year-old who refuses to revise for her GCSEs or how to convince your teenagers to volunteer more personal information about their days. This book is about one thing: equipping us, as we are right now, to confidently enable our teenagers to have a vibrant, two-way relationship with the God who loves them.

My prayer is that this book helps you find your next steps in seeing your children grow in their connection with God. May God, our Father, give you sleep, stamina and grace as you go on this brilliant adventure of parenting with him.

- 1 -

THE PLACE OF PARENTS

The life of teenagers is beautiful and complicated. Throughout this season, teenagers are exploring who they are and what they believe. They are examining how the world works and their place in it. They are making choices and mistakes and learning how relationships function. It is a messy, significant time of growth for them, and through it all, they are on an ever-changing journey of faith.

If we want our children to embrace a life of faith during this season, we need to empower them to meaningfully connect with God through a two-way relationship with him. We'll call this being 'God-connected'.

You may have encountered a teen you would recognise as being 'God-smart'. This teen would know the standard Bible stories and rules for Christian living and be familiar with the routines of a church service. They are comfortable with how to do Christianity, but it all seems to stop at their head. It doesn't seem to make a difference in how they see themselves or how they interact with the world or with God.

A teen who is God-connected, on the other hand, seems to have something that goes beyond head-knowledge. A teen who is God-connected lives in a vibrant two-way relationship with God. They share life with him and interact with him throughout the day. They know they are loved and handle the world with the confidence that comes from having the peace and healing of the living God in their daily reality. Their head-knowledge of God is a part of discovering a lifelong heart-connection with him.

Our hearts long to help our teens be God-connected, but we can often feel trapped into only helping them be God-smart, hoping that one day they'll wake up and be magically God-connected. It can make us feel like powerless spectators cheering on our teens in their faith journeys from the outside. But that's not God's plan for us.

God's plan

God has a plan for how to create God-connected tweens and teenagers, and it may come as a bit of a surprise.

> Listen, Israel! The Lord our God is the only true God! So love the Lord your God with all your heart, soul, and strength. Memorise his laws and tell them to your children over and over again. Talk about them all the time, whether you're at home or walking along the road or going to bed at night, or getting up in the morning. Write down copies and tie them to your wrists and foreheads to help you obey them. Write these laws on the door frames of your homes and on your town gates.
>
> DEUTERONOMY 6:4–9 (CEV)

It appears that God's plan for teenagers to learn how to connect with him happens during the most boring parts of life when *we are with them*. Look at the passage again. The prime time for our children to learn about God is in the ordinary moments we have together with them: when we are at home in our pyjamas eating breakfast cereal and staring off into space; while we are sprawled around the house looking at our phones and tablets; as we are busily cooking an evening meal; when we are checking in on our teen doing homework or preparing for bed; while we are getting dressed in a panic for church; or even

It appears that God's plan for teenagers to learn how to connect with him happens during the most boring parts of life when we are with them.

when we are enduring those eye-pokingly boring car journeys together.

We spend on average around 2,000 hours a year with our teenagers. That's a lot of time together. So if we want our children to know how to access God in everyday life, then they need to experience it happening in *their* everyday life – with us, where we are. That is how God designed it. In these ordinary, everyday places teens learn *with us* how to find God in a complex world, and they discover *with us* how to walk with him in the ups and downs that come in life. Teenagers need people to walk alongside them in their spiritual exploration and help them as they grow in their understanding of who God is and how to engage with him in a complicated world. We get to be those people for our teenagers.

What about the church?

Church leaders have no access to those ordinary places with our families. Our youth leaders don't wake up in our houses to make breakfast or take our teens to dance classes. They don't stand bored in a queue with us or stand in our teen's doorways listening to them describe the latest adaptions to their favourite online game. The church, it seems, isn't in places that God has designed for teenagers' discipleship to happen.

Yes, the church community is a wonderful and important factor in a teen's spiritual life. It provides a broader range of faith-filled voices speaking truth. It can be a place of acceptance and encouragement, a community for them to explore their power and significance, and a raft of affirmation for their growing independence and identity. The church can offer Christian peers, intergenerational relationships and a gathering point to learn about God and encounter him.

There are many places in this book where we talk about helping teenagers engage with the church. But the church isn't meant to be the centre of our teenager's spiritual life, because the church only spends about 100 hours a year with them during all-together events.

That doesn't mean, however, that we are alone. In biblical times, when God instructed Moses on how the next generation could find connection with him, parents were part of close-knit extended families. Those extended families were part of a wider clan, and those clans were part of a tribe of people. No parent was on their own. In modern times, we can often feel the loss of that community. Not all of us have a Christian extended family or community that supports us.

It is important that you know the church is behind you, is for you, is cheering you on and is the community you can rely on. Other Christian parents will have your back, and there are people of all ages in your church who are willing to surround you, love you and help you on this journey. They can't do the job for you, but they can make sure you aren't doing it alone. And they can be the extended family of love and encouragement for you and your children. We as parents were never designed to be parenting for faith alone, and if you don't have that community around you, please link yourself into a church and let some people know that you need it.

The aim of this book

Research studies repeatedly affirm that parents are the primary influencer of their teenagers' faith journeys. How we influence just may look different now than when our children were younger. Parenting is a journey that never ends. It simply transforms through the years. What our babies needed from us back then is different than what our tweenagers need from us now. What our teens need from us now will be different from what our 40-year-old adult children will need from us in the future. In every stage, we are needed and valuable, and we have influence and significance, especially in helping our children meet and know God. We, as parents and carers, are anything but powerless.

But many of us can feel hesitant when it comes to wading into our children's faith journeys. Some of us worry that we don't know how to do it well. Others of us worry about damaging our children's faith or pushing them away from God accidentally if we are too proactive about it. Some of us feel like our teenagers will shut down or shut us out. The aim of this book is to give you the approaches, skills and confidence to help your teenagers flourish spiritually. Your family is unique. It is different from everyone else's. You are the expert on your children and your family. You will be able to adapt everything to the way your family works best.

Wherever you are now in your relationship with your child, wherever your child is now in their relationship with God, know that this is only one moment in a long faith journey. Today, your teen may be rejecting God or may be fully and happily connected with him. But tomorrow will be different as they experience the next step on their faith journey. We have a significant opportunity to help our teenagers in their faith journey today, and what they learn in this season will stay with them for a lifetime. This book will help you embrace this season, these opportunities, in whatever it looks like for you and your teenagers.

Over the next chapters, we will look at how we can journey alongside our children's faith well, helping them find their next step with God. We will explore how we can equip our teenagers to find God in their daily lives, discovering their own patterns of connection with him, and to navigate their purpose and grow in confidence in a world that doesn't know him. My hope is that each chapter will give you new ways of seeing and understanding your teens' relationship with God and give you more tools to your parenting bag and for you to use or not use as you feel is right.

– 2 –

THE POWER OF WINDOWS

A long time ago, I was a junior part-time youth secretary at a large church led by our senior pastor, Jim. He was a fantastic leader – incredibly kind, very humble, pastoral and wise, everything you could ever want in a church leader. He oozed Jesus. I loved being part of his crowd. I was one of 40 or so staff, and I felt so included, even as he would laugh with the senior team at the other end of the staff room. I got to shout, 'Hi!' with our group of administrators as he popped his head into our busy office each day. I loved hearing him preach and listening to all the stories about his family. He prayed for me once, with about 150 other people, at the end of a service. He was my leader, I belonged to his crowd, and I loved it.

And then the incident happened. It was at the annual staff retreat. After three days of visionary talks and enormous amounts of food, it was time to head home. Several of us from the admin team ran off for a last swim in the hotel pool. On the way back to our rooms to get changed to leave (there was no changing room at the pool), my friends thought it would be funny to leave me dripping in the hotel lobby while they ran ahead to take the lift without me.

As I waited for the lift to come back down, a puddle forming around me on the marble floor despite the four towels and robe I was wearing over my swimming costume, I saw them – the senior leadership team. They were walking out of the front door leaving our leader Jim behind in the lobby with just me and the hotel staff. He saw me and began to walk over, probably out of concern for me, as I looked like a drowned rat.

I panicked, because at that moment I realised something. I had comfortably been part of his crowd for five years, and yet I had never had a one-to-one conversation with him. I had no idea how to talk to this leader that I so respected.

My brain caught fire. 'What do I do? What do I do? Do I explain? Act casual? Ask a theological question? Tell him how much I want to be like him when I grow up? Would that be weird? Should I tell him my name? Wait, he should know my name. *What if he doesn't know my name?* What if I tell him and he's insulted that I assumed he didn't know? Aargh!'

He was looking at me expectantly, and I realised that while I was screaming in my head, he had spoken to me.

'I've been swimming,' I blurted out.

'I can see that,' he said kindly as the lift doors opened and I dashed away. I was horrified and baffled. I felt like I had known my leader well, since I had been part of his crowd for so long. But when faced with a situation where I needed to talk with him, I froze. I realised how far apart we actually were and how little relationship really existed between us.

Many of our children feel the same way about God because their time to engage with him is usually in 'together' environments. We go to church together, where we sing and talk together about God. At youth group, teens listen to talks about God together and pray for each other. When our children were smaller, we may have prayed or read the Bible together at bedtime. Over the years, our teens have become used to being a part of God's crowd.

Then one day we turn to our kids and say, 'You can have your own special one-to-one relationship with the God of the universe, who is powerful beyond all things. Good luck!' And we leave them alone to figure out how to embark on an individual journey with him. Many teenagers have no idea how to make that leap on their own.

If we want our children to learn how to have their own individual connection with God, they need to be equipped in how to walk with God in a personal way through the ups and downs of normal life. That's where we come in.

Our children learn how relationships work from watching us in our relationships. They watch and see how we behave with others and what we expect from them. They observe the impact people have on us and the value we place on them in our lives.

Our children see how, when we are stressed, we turn to our friends for advice and connection. They hear us laughing together and get a sense of the joy our friendships bring us. They know how we prioritise helping our friends and the time we give to them. Through this experience of watching, listening and participating, they learn what to look for in a friend and how to be a friend to others. They are aware that our friendships go deeper than they can see, but they learn to watch and listen for the benefits of those friendships to us and the way we choose to commit our lives to them. Whether it's our friendships or relationships with our partners or work colleagues, our children are always learning from the little glimpses of these connections that we show them.

We don't fling open the doors and give our children all-access passes to view the intimate details of our marriage or friendships, but we do try to show them the 'tip of the iceberg' of what these healthy relationships are. Only ten per cent of an iceberg is above water. We cannot see how big an iceberg is under the surface, but we can get an indication from how much we see above it. It is the same with our relationships.

The problem is that we rarely allow our children similar access to our relationship with God. It can be utterly foreign to them. They often know what we believe and that our beliefs steer our lives, but they don't often get to see how our relationship with God works and in what ways it affects who we are and how we live our lives.

God has positioned us perfectly so we can show our children an up-close view of what life with God looks like day to day, messy bits and all. When our children can see, hear and learn how our relationship with God affects our every day, then they can begin to explore what it looks like for them.

If we want our children to connect heart-to-heart with God and gain their identity and purpose from him in a living and active relationship, we need to show them the many tips of the icebergs that exist in our relationship with him. We need to learn how to do bits of our private relationship in a public sphere.

It's not about having the 'ideal' relationship with God

At this point, if you're like me, fear begins to creep in – my relationship with God isn't the ideal that I want my children to be looking at. We all know ourselves. We know our flaws, our sins, our imperfections, our laziness, our weaknesses and our strengths. The idea of using our internal relationship with God as a key influence in our children's lives can be scary and make us feel exposed.

I vividly remember a conference speaker once saying, as she leaned casually on her podium, 'Well, I just tell parents to be Jesus to your children, and as you are Jesus to your children, they will see him and want to be with him.' The full force of that hit me in the chest. I thought, 'If my child's relationship with God is based on my ability to be Jesus and reflect him perfectly, then my child doesn't have a chance! I am not that good yet. I am trying, but if my child's future faith is dependent on my ability to reflect Jesus accurately at all times, it will never happen.'

Luckily, that isn't the truth. That isn't why God put us in our children's lives. Jesus is the only perfect one we can model our lives on. What we offer our teenagers is an invitation to journey through life with God alongside us.

We aren't trying to pass on our faith to our children – we want them to find their own way with God, however it looks for them. But we can be a slightly more experienced companion on the journey. We are co-travellers with our children on life's journey of faith. As our children journey through life in connection with God, they can look over at us to see how to negotiate the obstacles of life with God. They can see how we hold his hand during the joyful bits and how we let him carry us during the hard bits. They can learn how to go on their own journey with him, by seeing the tip of the iceberg of how we do ours. Teens don't want someone to control their process and instruct them to have faith in the 'right way'. They want to find their own path, but that doesn't mean they don't want help.

> They want to find their own path, but that doesn't mean they don't want help.

If we show them only that life is great, that we always pray and are always perfect, and that God wants us to be happy, then we're setting them up to be disappointed in themselves and the Christian walk. We're setting them up to feel like they're failing when they experience the downs within the many ups. I want my child to be able to handle anything in life, positive and negative, because they are walking with God. And at times we will look at the tip of our child's iceberg of their relationship with God and will learn some things too.

All we need to be is on the journey. When we're on the journey and they're on the journey, it's exciting because we get to walk together.

Create windows

Have you ever walked down a road of terraced houses? We used to live on such a street, and I loved looking into other people's windows. My husband said that doing so was rude – the net curtains hanging in the window meant, 'Don't look in my house.' I disagreed. What I found most fascinating was how, even though the houses all had the same footprint as ours, the inside of each one looked vastly different. Some people had three sofas; others had only two armchairs. Some floors were carpeted; others were wooden. Some people had knocked out walls; others had extended to make space for a kitchen in the back. I loved walking along and exclaiming, 'Oh, look at that. What a good idea!'; 'Oh no, I don't like that'; 'Hmm, we could try one of those bamboo screens. Very clever.'

People observe each other all the time. Most of the significant things I've learned about life with God, I've learned from watching other people and getting a window into their lives. Our children need us to open some windows into aspects of our relationship with God so they can see what life with God can look like.

To our teenagers, our relationship with God may be shrouded in mystery. We attend prayer meetings, but they stay at home. We read our Bible on our phone, but they never see it. We desperately pray for them in our minds as they head to yet another party, but they never hear us. We agonise with God about the right decision at work, but they never know about it. We may be broken and grieving from losing our friend, but they never understand how God is daily comforting and speaking with us about it.

When our teens cannot see our faith journey, they may make huge assumptions. They may assume that God isn't relevant in our daily life or that our faith is centred in simple church activity. They may not imagine how God is involved in our everyday emotions and decisions. They need us to create little windows into our life with God so they can see the possibilities.

Our teenagers are looking to see what an authentic life with God looks like, not a perfect life. We, as parents, can sometimes feel the pressure to spiritually perform for our children, to be good role models for them. My suggestion would be that what teens need most, what they crave most, is for someone to show them the reality of the ups and downs of life *with* God in it. They need to see how to engage with God in good times and bad, and how to wrestle with ethical difficulties and tough decisions. Our teenagers want to know how to engage with God when we sin or make mistakes, struggle with our mental health or live with blessings when others seem to have less.

> *Our teenagers are looking to see what an authentic life with God looks like.*

If our children cannot see God in ordinary life, then when they experience questions or doubts they have no framework for how to continue walking with him. What does someone do with God when they are struggling in prayer, or when they are hurt or disappointed? What do they do when they are grateful for God's faithfulness? Or what about when they sin or feel they're a failure and don't know how to break free from the shame and guilt? Our teens need authentic adults living genuine faith alongside them, so they can watch and learn and create their own authentic life with the God of the universe. Our imperfections as ordinary humans on a faith journey give our teens permission to be imperfect ordinary humans on their own lifetime journey with a perfect God.

So how do we do this well? Here are three ways to get started: let them see it while it's happening; tell stories; and ask opinions.

Let them see it while it's happening

Let your teens see brief windows into what *your* normal life with God looks like now. There is no pressure to display what it *should* look like or what you want it to look like for *them*. The key to creating windows is to allow little glimpses into the various aspects of your personal relationship with God so that your teenagers can see what it looks like to be involved in a two-way connection with an invisible person.

Leave the door ajar when you spend time with God, so they can see that you aren't floating four inches off the ground surrounded by white light. (If you are doing that, it will certainly function as a conversation starter later!) Let them hear you singing along to worship songs in the kitchen or mumbling a prayer to God as you drive past a car accident. If you read your Bible or listen to it on audiobook, occasionally let them see or hear you doing it. If you love worshipping at church or home, let it flow. If you read Christian books and write in them, leave them out so your teens can snoop and see what you think. Seeing a person engage with God is fascinating, and it's even more so if that person is your parent.

Creating windows isn't just about the distinctly spiritual things we do. Our children need windows into all areas of our lives with God. I know one family that went through a big move and the son was struggling to settle into his new school. His dad shared with his son that he understood because he felt the same way about his own new workplace. He told his son that he felt the need to pray for help every morning as he started work and how God was helping him.

If you are chatting with your friends about God and life, let your teens stay in the room when you talk about anxiety or discouragement or as you share what God has been teaching you in this season. When I was a teenager, my parents and their friends would occasionally invite me into their conversations. I'm sure I only heard a bit of what was really going on, but I was at the dinner table and sitting in the lounge with them as they discussed job losses, health struggles and theological problems. I heard of how one friend was processing her recent life-altering diagnosis with God and how another was annoyed at the latest sermon and what he disagreed with based on his experience with God and how he read scripture. I saw my dad praying for his friends and mum highlighting scripture that would help as she conversed on the sofa. This experience taught me so much about the friendships I wanted and how to find God in all sorts of life issues. When we give our teens windows into where God is in our lives *as it happens*, we show them the vitality of the kind of life with God they can have.

Most of the time, teenagers are completely unaware of how big a role our relationship with God plays in our daily lives, particularly in terms of how we overcome struggles, reach decisions and handle hurt. In part, this is because we rightly wish to protect our children. We are the parents, and we are not to burden them with our problems. We can want to shield our children from our emotions so they don't take on responsibility that isn't theirs to care for us or try to help us. We want to be the steady, safe, rock-solid person for our teens, especially in their chaotic season of teen life. But if we never model how to conquer those problems, they won't have a framework to learn how to do the hard bits of life with God for themselves.

A helpful rule of thumb to remember so that we don't feel worried about oversharing is to create a window *for a purpose*. We aren't dropping our boundaries and making our children pastorally care for us through our difficulties. We can choose to be strategic about it and decide for ourselves when our children get to see those honest bits of our lives. We give them glimpses because we want to give them a window into how to walk this part of life *with God*. So the windows we create are not just our emotions or situations, but they are windows into how we cope with those situations with God.

If you are annoyed at a colleague at work for lying to you, create a window into that. You can share how you are in a tricky situation at work and trying to figure out what to do. You can create windows into how you were out jogging and just spent the whole time ranting at God about the situation, or how you tried praying for the person in the shower because you realised you just got stuck in resenting them. You can share how you asked God for wisdom before you went into a meeting, or how God had been poking you to love them.

Our mistakes also become beautiful windows our children can see into. Many parents have confided in me about their anger difficulties and how ashamed they sometimes feel after they yell at their children. I encourage them to help their children see how to work that out with God. Why not go to your teen and say, 'I'm so sorry I yelled. That was wrong of me. I always want to have God's love and peace in my heart, but today I was tired and exhausted, and I let my frustration come out as anger at you. I'm sorry. Please forgive me. I'm not perfect yet; God is still working on me. I will get better!'

Even our disappointments can be helpful for our kids. For example, you could say, 'I don't know how you feel, but I can sometimes feel disappointed when something I prayed for doesn't seem to have happened. I've been telling God all about it, because I wanted him to rescue my job, but I still got made redundant. You know how I've been dealing with it? I keep reminding myself that it says in the Bible that he works in all things for our good. So I keep telling him, "Okay, God, I'm looking for all the good stuff that you are going to do!"'

Tell stories

We have a wealth of experiences that may be helpful for our teens to hear as they consider where God is in their circumstances and how to connect with him. We can share these stories of our experience as part of our general conversation throughout the day, or in response to a particular situation. One dad told me how he was able to help his teenage son through a nasty break-up. He said to his son, 'I remember when my first girlfriend broke up with me. I thought she was the one. I just sat on my bed and cried – no, seriously, really cried hard. Best time I ever had with God, just me crying on a bed and knowing he was in the room with me. He didn't talk to me or show me anything, but it was so nice to feel him in the room while my heart was all torn up, and know he was there for me. I don't think I talked to anyone for a week. But I got through it, very slowly. I believe in you, son.'

Teens face some big decisions in their lives, friendships, and schooling. They need to hear stories of how we made important decisions. Share stories of how you knew you should propose to your partner or how you chose to leave a job. How did God lead or help you? What type of conversations did you have with God about it? We can share stories of things that went well or ones that had catastrophic endings. The point isn't that we were perfect, but that God was there helping us through it all.

You can even share stories of your teenager's past from your unique perspective. As they get older, you may want to share the story of their illness when they were two and where God was helping them and you through the fears of hospital visits and surgeries. Or share with your disappointed sixth former after exams about that time when she was eight and you lost your job, and how you and your family struggled to find a new future and how God helped.

Ask opinions

Teens are growing in their view of the world, and as a result, some teens have a lot of opinions. One way to help them engage with who God is in the everyday is to invite their opinion into your situations. You can be walking to the shop and say, 'Can I ask for your opinion? I was listening to a podcast and this person said this thing about God that I'm not sure about. I went to the verses in the Bible they were talking about, and am not sure I agree with the way they interpret those verses. What do you think?' Outline what you are wrestling with, get their opinion and appreciate what they added. This helps you get insight into what your teen thinks, and you've created a window into how you and all people of faith can wrestle with ideas and continue to learn. With this knowledge of their opinion, you can then create new windows or experiences to help them explore God's heart in the situation.

The pattern of Jesus

Remember, these windows exist to allow our teenagers access to the way our lives entwine with God the Father in relationship, and to show them what it looks like when that happens. Jesus was a master at doing this with his disciples, who may have also been teenagers and young adults, according to many scholars.

Jesus taught his disciples not to publicise their giving to the temple, their prayers or their fasting. He taught them to keep these activities between them and God, not between them and the world's approval (Matthew 6:1–18). But this didn't mean that he hid everything from them. He built windows into his private life with his Father, so that his disciples had a front-row view whenever he chose to give them a glimpse. They knew his habits of fasting and prayer (Matthew 14:23) and his patterns of giving (Matthew 17:24–27), and they overheard his prayers well enough to write them down later (John 17). Jesus wasn't allowing them that access so that the disciples would huddle around saying, 'Wow! Jesus is amazing. He is the best pray-er I've ever heard. And isn't he holy? I mean, very impressive, really.' He gave them those tip-of-the-iceberg moments so that they could learn a new way of interacting with God their heavenly Father, in relationship, not just as part of the crowd.

Of course, Jesus is our perfect example of how to create windows into the heart of God and a relationship with him. He showed us parents the way we could do it. And even though our own journey with God will be imperfect, our two-way relationship with him can always be *authentic*. That's how God designed us.

Teenagers are naturally watching us all the time, and they see our imper-fections, especially in areas of faith. At times we can feel as if our teens are the

> Teenagers are naturally watching us all the time, and they see our imperfections, especially in areas of faith.

hypocrisy police: watching our behaviour and trying to assess whether we live what we say we believe. Their attention can feel intrusive or annoying sometimes, but their natural tendency works fantastically to our advantage. It can feel painful when our teens point out our flaws or our failings to live up to our own ideals. But it is *only* stressful if we hold ourselves up to a perfect standard. It can be a gift to them if, when they see a discrepancy between our professed faith and our choices, we are able to say, 'I know, I seem to be struggling with this. I'm working on it, and God's working on it. I'm so glad that God has grace for my mess-ups because I can sure beat myself up about them.' If we can create windows into being on a faith journey, we can free our teens from the spiral of shame and worry that many can feel when holding themselves up to a perfect spiritual standard.

Helping teenagers' faith journeys can sometimes be a slow burn. Sometimes you will feel impactful in the moment and see almost immediate benefits in your children's lives. There are also times where you may wonder, 'Is any of this going in? Is there any point in this?' I guarantee you the answer is yes! Our teens may be quietly storing away all they see and hear from us about God. They may be chewing it over. They may implement it right away, or they may pull it out and dust it off years later, and use it then. As a youth leader, over and over again I have seen teenagers refer back to specific things they saw in their parent's walks with God years before and say that they tried it that week and it was fantastic.

You can use every part of your authentic life with God to equip your teens for the entirety of their lives. Parenting for faith is simply asking yourself, 'How can I help my teen take their next step on their journey of faith?' For many, creating windows may be one way to provide for your teen's next step.

- 3 -

TYING TOGETHER TRUTH AND EXPERIENCE

Gwynneth ran out of the Sunday group room and slammed the door behind her. Her three-year-old brother had just died, and her world had been turned upside down. When I caught up with her, she scowled at me. 'I know all of this stuff!' she said, waving her arms. 'It's not like any of it matters anyway. I memorised these stupid verses and I've heard the story of Noah a billion times. And don't tell me God loves me, blah blah blah. It doesn't mean anything!' Tears poured down Gwynneth's face and her whole body shook with anger. She so needed to connect with God's comfort and love, but none of her knowledge was helping her find him.

Moments of need often expose the cracks in our faith. Gwynneth realised how disconnected she actually was from God when she discovered her knowledge of him couldn't help her when she needed him the most. What she really needed was a relationship with God, and she didn't have it. But a relationship with God isn't just for crisis points; it's for every moment of every day. When we live in relationship with God, we can access all he has for us all the time: his joy, his guidance, his companionship, his strength and power, his love and truth. Within that relationship, God helps us and sustains us through all the good and bad times of our lives.

To help our teenagers develop a relationship with God, we need to look at how good relationships develop. Relationships require many things, two of which are knowledge and experience. People who read my CV may gain some knowledge about me, but they still want to meet me in an interview to match that knowledge with the experience of knowing me in a relationship. Other people might first meet me casually at a party or conference and then later want to deepen that experience by meeting up to gain more knowledge about me. This is how we, as humans, build and maintain relationships. When we grow in our knowledge and experience of people, we also grow closer and deeper in relationship with them. Eventually, we might add in personal commitments to extend that process of discovery, and voila – we're on the road to developing and maintaining deep, connected friendships and relationships.

God meant our relationship with him to work in the same way – because *knowledge about him* and *experience of him* go hand in hand. When a teacher of the law asked which commandment was the most important, Jesus replied, 'The most important one says: "People of Israel, you have only one Lord and God. You must love him with all your heart, soul, mind, and strength"' (Mark 12:29–30, CEV). This is a holistic way of loving, involving everything in us – our emotions, our will and our understanding – in which all aspects of love are tied together.

We also see our teenagers tie together knowledge and experience as they work out their relationship with us. We tell them that we love them, but they want to match this knowledge with experiences to see if it is true. They want to know if we still love them when they are disruptive or disappointing or when they fail. They test out the truth of our love and eventually grow to feel secure in it. Their experience of relationship with us matches the truth of our love, and the truth of our love is made evident in their experience.

Too often, we don't allow our children to go through the same process with God. We feed them information about God but don't guide them to experience the truth of it in relationship, so they have no experience to match it to. Conversely, if they have an experience with God, we might forget to guide them to the biblical truth behind that encounter, so they have no truth to anchor their experience. This happens to us as adults, as well. When truth and experience aren't tied together, we try to make sense of it on its own, which often leads to forming wrong assumptions about God and our relationship with him.

Problems when biblical truth is not tied to experience

If teenagers know biblical truth but haven't been guided to see how that truth fits in with their experiences with God, they often make wrong assumptions about how their relationship with God works. These wrong assumptions often become the prime reasons tweens and teens struggle with their faith. For example:

- **Biblical truth:** God has a plan (Jeremiah 29:11).
- **Wrong relational assumption:** Everything that happens to me is part of God's plan, and I shouldn't do anything until I am sure that it is part of his plan.

- **Biblical truth:** God is loving (Psalm 42:8; 57:3; John 3:16).
- **Wrong relational assumption:** Nothing bad should happen to me or anyone I love because God loves me.

- **Biblical truth:** God knows everything (Psalm 147:4–5; Acts 15:16–18).
- **Wrong relational assumption:** I don't have to tell God how I feel or share anything with him in prayer because he knows everything already.

As we see, there can be a vast difference between our children's wrong assumptions and the following ways God designed our relationships with him to work:

- God has wonderful plans for us that we can choose to take part in. He also gave us free will, as well as desires and dreams for our lives which he wants to bless (Psalm 37:4).

- God loves us, but his love doesn't mean that he puts us in a bubble to isolate us from the world. It means that he is committed to being in relationship with us, comforting, guiding, strengthening and encouraging us as we walk with him through life. Things will go wrong in our lives that he didn't cause, and we will make poor choices that affect us badly, but, because he loves us, he promises that he will work them together for our good (Romans 8:28).

- Although God knows everything about us – our thoughts, our hearts, our actions – he has forged a way for us to have a relationship with him, even sacrificing his Son, because he longs for us to want to share our lives with him in a two-way relationship.

No wonder many of our teenagers struggle with their faith when their knowledge of God leads them to wrong expectations about their experience with him, which then disconnect them from God and result in disappointment. The truth they know should be drawing them *closer* into relationship with him as they see it reflected in their experience. We can help our teens tie their knowledge *about* God to their experiences *of* him.

Problems when experience is not tied to biblical truth

If we simply validate children's experiences and perceptions of God without grounding them in biblical truth, we are enabling them to invent 'truth' out of their experience.

When I was a child, my mum always made me eat the crusts on my sandwiches. Based on my experience – that this was important to my mother and that crusts had an unappealing taste – I assumed some 'truths' about crusts. I believed that the crust of the bread held more nutrients than the rest of it. The more types of bread I saw and tasted, the more I felt confirmed in my belief. I passed this 'truth' on to the children I worked with, and I insisted it was true when I talked with my friends. I would even force myself to eat crusts to ensure I was benefitting from all the nutrients in them. Embarrassingly, I made it to the age of 26 before I discovered that my assumed truths about bread crusts were not, in fact, true!

Although this may seem like a silly example, it illustrates how easily we can encourage an experience and leave out the underlying truth that goes with it. As parents we may do the same by encouraging too much experience of God without tying it into biblical truth. When we leave truth out, children will draw their own assumptions, which will often be wrong, and then they'll apply those assumptions to other aspects of their relationship with God, as well. For example:

- **Experience:** Some people hear God speak occasionally.
- **Wrong truth assumption:** God doesn't speak very often. His speech is very unpredictable. And if he speaks to others and not much to me, then he must be cross with me or doesn't care about me.

- **Experience:** My world is falling apart.
- **Wrong truth assumption:** God has abandoned me or is punishing me.

- **Experience:** I had a wonderful time with God at the church retreat/conference/camp.
- **Wrong truth assumption:** It was a 'mountaintop' experience, which doesn't happen in the everyday world.

These kinds of experiences are very poignant and very real to teenagers, but, if no one helps them connect their experiences to biblical truths, they may create assumed truths that aren't found in the Bible. Assumed truths lead to wrong views of God and result in a disconnected relationship with him. Real biblical truths lead to a rooting in God that guides, informs and increases a healthy relationship with him, as in the following:

- God is constantly speaking to us, and he promises that we will grow to recognise and know his voice (Jeremiah 33:3; Job 33:13–14; John 10:2–5, 14–15).

- He promises to be with us and walk with us through our struggles, comforting and encouraging us (Psalm 23).

- We can experience his presence and closeness every day, and we can enjoy him wherever we are, in whatever circumstance (John 14:16; Matthew 28:20).

Many teens struggle because they need help to measure and deepen their experience with God by rooting those experiences into biblical truth. We can help them do that.

Practical ways of tying together biblical truth and experience

To grow healthy relationships, we need a good balance of truth and relational experience. It is important that we learn to wrap one around the other, viewing one in the context of the other, so they become inextricably linked.

To grow healthy relationships, we need a good balance of truth and relational experience.

Let's look at four methods we can use to help our teens tie together truth and experience:

- explain the world
- answer their questions
- answer their hidden questions
- lay a framework for future seasons.

Explain the world

As our children grow older, we sometimes forget that they still have questions. They still need us to help them understand the world of friendships, politics, perseverance, pain and joy. They still have those internal *why* questions. They often just don't ask them.

We can get ahead of our teens' questions by explaining the world *as we go about our day*, rather than waiting for them to find the words and the boldness to ask a question.

> As our children grow older, we sometimes forget that they still have questions.

Our teenagers need our help in understanding the world with God in it, and in working out how to engage with him in response. This is important because faith and relationship with God often get isolated somehow from real life. When we explain things well, we can reconnect them. But too often we don't explain things well and instead give a short, disconnected answer: 'We go to church because this is what we do as a Christian family'; 'Sex before marriage is wrong because that's what it says in the Bible.' When we only lay down boundaries and rules, our teens are left with a simple response of obey or not, agree or reject. If we want our children to truly engage with God, we need to explain the *why* underneath the rule so they can grow in understanding who God is, why he says what he does and how that impacts how we engage with the world.

Let's explain the *why* of church: 'Church is one of the biggest gifts God gives us, because it is a family of people who mutually commit to loving and encouraging each other, empowering each other to use their gifts and being challenged to walk with God. We go to church to meet with God together. We go because we are needed, and we go because we need to be a part of it.' The *why* behind church can open conversations about the purpose behind church, not just the behaviour we want our children to conform to.

Let's explain the *why* of sex: 'Sex is an amazing thing that God created, and science has shown how significant sex is, physiologically and psychologically, to us and to our relationships. I'd love to explore more with you about why God talks about sex a lot in the Bible and what that means for how we live life.' Your *why* behind God's purposes for sex and how you want your teen to think about it and view it will invite discussion and questions that will shape their faith-filled view of relationships going forward.

You are the parents, the experts in your own children. When you explain the *whys*, use your knowledge of your teens to do so in ways they can understand and at the pace and depth they are interested in, just as you do about any other topic. This is especially powerful when we get to help our teenagers tie emotional experiences to the truths of who God is and help them see how to walk with him in it.

Take another example – a terminally ill grandparent. Our teens know that God is loving, but they often struggle to figure out what that means when Grandma is dying from a stroke. Our children know about prayer, but they get confused about *why* God didn't do what they wanted him to do. Since a lot of the spiritual problems happen when teens are left to make those connections on their own, we need to help them along. We can wade in and say, 'Sometimes it's hard to see what God is doing and to know what to expect. God promises in the Bible that he responds to our prayers, and I trust that he is doing things. I may be able to see it, and I may not. Sometimes that is frustrating to me. But, I'm learning how to look for what he *is* doing rather than get annoyed that he *isn't* doing the one thing I want. When I see Grandma, I see that God sits with her in hospital when we can't. I know that he loves her more than I do. I believe he is helping her in ways I will never know. Last night she slept peacefully, and I thank God for giving her that. I don't know why he's not just miraculously healing her, but I do see him doing things. How do you feel about it?'

Or take sung worship in church services, for instance. When we are in a church gathering, we can easily assume our teenagers know what is going on. We can forget that they might not understand as much as we think, and maybe they've already formed some wrong assumptions about it. Sung worship can often look like a big group sing-song with no real purpose, and we may have forgotten along the way to explain to our teenagers *why* we sing to an invisible God and how it works. You might say, 'I'm never quite sure what to do when we sing because I can't follow the words that fast, so I just close my eyes and listen because I find the words encouraging. They remind me of truths about God that I often don't think about.' Or, 'I tend to sing all the words because I want to mean them all, and sometimes worship is about letting my heart be brave enough to say these things to God, no matter what I'm feeling today. It makes me feel connected to him.'

My dad was a police officer, and I would often wake up at 2.00 am, after he came home at the end of a shift, and see him reading his Bible at the kitchen table. I would watch him read, nod and write notes on a pad beside his Bible. He was a parent who naturally created windows into his life, so he would leave his notes out, and in the morning I would often read them. My love of scripture started there.

But one day when I was 14, he saw me reading his notes and he told me, 'You know some days are really hard. I go to a call where I have to hold a dead baby or take a report from a raped teenager. I come home and feel emotionally exhausted.' He then reached forward and touched his Bible. 'Reading the Bible fills me up and nails it all down. Everything I see, everything I do and everything I feel just gets nailed down to the truth that never changes when I read it. I really need it.'

Whack! That moment seared into my brain. Anytime I read the Bible, anytime I see anyone read the Bible, that phrase comes back to me. The way he said it slammed everything into place for me, and I understood what scripture was for and I knew I wanted to engage with it.

Let's look at one more example. When you decide to sell the family car, for instance, you can give your teen the short answer, 'We are going to sell the car', or you can show them the actual process you went through with God to make that decision:

> I'm so sorry I've been stressed a lot. The car keeps having things wrong with it, and I've been so 'argh' about it all. I kept going on and on and on to God about how frustrated I was. But he soon told me that I was stressed because I didn't trust he would help, even though he had helped so many times before. God was right. I *can* trust him. So I've made a decision. We are going to sell the car. I am grateful for this car and for how long we've had it. We'll see what God does next. He may provide a car, he may give us the means to pay for one, or we may be in a season of finding new ways to get to places. But I do trust that God will provide what we need.

When we show our teens our decision-making process, they begin to see how the truth they see in the Bible, and how we experience that truth in our daily lives, are tied together. Whether it's while we are watching TV at night or dealing with a broken boiler, we have constant opportunities to frame for our children how to understand suffering, friendships, purpose and, most of all, who God is in the swirl of life around us. Because God isn't a separate addition to the side of life. God is a significant part of all of it.

But if you're like me, you may have a creeping worry forming in the corner of your mind: 'I'm still learning how to live life with God. I'm not sure I know enough to explain all these things to my teen right now. I still have a lot of questions.' If that's you, you don't need to worry. Give your teen as much as you have right now. And as you grow in

God, you'll be able to share new insights with them. You can even discover new things together. As long as you are on the journey, you are on the right track, and you have a community around you to help encourage you.

Answer their questions

Addressing teens' questions goes beyond helping them find the biblical answer. It's about creating a culture where questions are okay. It's about exploring ideas together and sharing the answers to the best of our ability, and knowing what to do when we need more information. Actually, how we handle not knowing the answer to a question can teach our teens just as much as answering the question.

Addressing teens' questions goes beyond helping them find the biblical answer. It's about creating a culture where questions are okay.

No matter what the question is, we can usually answer in this way:

- **What do you think?** Many times teenagers ask questions because they want to talk about something. If we allow them to answer first, then we can access what is in their hearts and minds, and hear what is worrying them.

- **What do we know?** We may know a little or we may know a lot, but sharing the truth as we understand it helps root our teenagers in biblical truth and experiences of God.

- **What do we not know?** There will be many things we don't know, but there are also many things theologians and scientists don't know either. It may be useful to say, 'You know what? I'm not even sure people who study these topics know the answer to that one!' or 'I don't know much about this topic, honestly.'

- **What does it look like for me and others?** In the end, how we as individuals work out this question in our own lives helps our teenagers see the impact it has on our walk with God and on others too. Create windows into how you've handled that question in your own life and the impact it has made.

For example, two huge questions that many of us were asking while I was writing this book were, 'Why didn't God stop the Covid-19 pandemic?' and 'What was he doing?' We can feel overwhelmed trying to answer those questions. But if the topic comes up and we don't address it, we would be missing a great opportunity. We could answer it like this:

- **What do you think?** 'Hmm, interesting question. What do you think?'

- **What do we know?** *Note: Everyone comes from different experiences and theological understandings. God has given you to your teen, so explain it according to the teachings that you hold. This is only one way of explaining it.* 'In the Bible I see that God tells us we will have trouble in this world. I think sin messed up the world, and death and pain came in. It happens to everybody, people who know God and people who don't, because we all live in this broken world. I know that sometimes God does miraculously intervene. I have seen it, and I know it. I know that God is compassionate, and he deeply loves each person. I know that God promises to be close to the brokenhearted, and there were a lot of those around. I know that God invites us to work with him to comfort and help those in need, and I know he comforts them himself too. I know God is the ultimate healer and creator, so I believe he was inspiring and helping doctors and scientists as they wrestled with it all. I know there won't be any pain or disease or loss in heaven, and so I am grateful that no matter what happens in this world, the next won't be like this. It will be better.'

- **What do we not know?** 'I don't know why God didn't stop this natural disaster from happening. But I also don't know how many natural disasters he has intervened in already. Maybe it would have been worse without God's help. I can't see all that God was doing. I only have a very narrow view of the pandemic.'

- **What does it look like for me?** 'When the pandemic hit, I wasn't too torn up with *why*, because I focused on how I could help. Sometimes we can get caught up in demanding that God answer why when that just traps my heart. God isn't accountable to me. I could never fully understand why he does or doesn't do something. But I know that he loves us and he's drawing people towards him and inviting me to help. My main question was, "God, what can I do to love people and help in this season?"'

You may have a totally different theological take on the pandemic. That's great! Explain how you and your church see it. You may have had a tough time wrestling with it yourself, so your answer will be more like, 'Honestly, I struggled with understanding why, so I just told God how I felt and tried to keep a conversation going with him through it all.'

If you genuinely have no idea about the answer, that is an excellent opportunity to say:

> What do you think? Very interesting. You know, I have never thought about this question before! What a great question. Let's see what the Bible says about that. Or let's do some research about it. Or we could call someone. Oh, let's call Annie and see what she thinks! She may have some valuable insights to help us understand more about it. That's what I do when I don't have an answer to a question. I know I can never know all the answers, which is why I'm glad I have wise friends who love God too and can help.

When we admit we don't know but we think it's important to find out, we are showing our teenagers that a relationship with God isn't about always knowing the correct answers or never doubting. It's about wondering and finding out and being okay with not knowing everything.

You may also occasionally give answers that you later disagree with. I have done this many times. When we give answers that we wish we hadn't, we can always come back the next day and say, 'Remember yesterday when I said that Jesus never talked about mental health? I was thinking more about it and I read an article online, and now I think I was wrong. I'll tell you what I found out…' Our teenagers will not be surprised that we can be wrong and that we're still learning, just as they are. They will be encouraged that being wrong and investigating to find answers is a normal part of life with God.

Giving a full answer like this will enable us to tie together the truth of God with our experiences of him, so our teens can see how we live our life and how he is inextricably woven into all of it.

Answer their hidden questions

Sometimes we can feel as if our teenagers are not interested in faith or God because we don't hear them talk about it. We may wonder how to answer questions they aren't asking out loud. Teens have different ways of communicating their questions. If we can learn to tune into those ways, we can help them engage with questions they don't yet know how to articulate.

Sometimes we can spot our teen's questions in what they disagree with. We may perceive their pushback against faith or God as a rejection, but I don't think that's the case. Often I find it's simply a way of communicating that they're struggling to tie together life and faith. They may be confused about how something in church applies to their current situation, or they may be experiencing something in life that they can't connect with their understanding of God.

Rather than get offended or rush to clarify the truth we see in scripture, take a few moments to ponder what questions your teen may be struggling with. Ask questions to understand them better. 'I hear you when you say you hate church. I wonder what it is about church that makes you feel uncomfortable? What annoys you about it and why? Tell me more about it because I want to see it from your perspective.' When we can draw those ideas out, we can begin to notice that they have some gaps in the *whys* of church or in how church applies to their life with God. Once we understand where they're coming from, we can help. It is best not to try to bring in our ideas at this moment, but merely accept their views and thank them for sharing with us what they think and feel. We have the information we need to understand what windows might be helpful to create, or what we want to frame for them the next time we talk about church. Our teenager's disagreements and pushbacks are useful communication through which we can hear and help them feel safe in talking to us about their concerns.

There are many ways we can spot our teenager's hidden questions. Sometimes it's in their disagreements or their passive resistance when they withdraw from activities. Other times it's in their vehement judgements of others, God or the church. It is all communication about what they are thinking and feeling, and if we can sidestep our emotions about it, we can understand our young people better and help them see how God and life are tied together. Chapter 7 will explore some tools for how to handle those conversations and clashes.

Lay a framework for future seasons

Sometimes life experiences can badly shake our belief in the reality of relationship with God. As adults, we can see some big issues coming, even if only a little bit ahead of time. It may be a family crisis, such as a divorce, bankruptcy, a big move, a death in the family or a loved one's illness. It may be a difficult life experience for our children, such as a new school, bullying, difficulty with reading or friendship issues.

If we know a difficult life experience is coming, we can prepare a solid, tied-together truth-and-experience spiritual framework for our teen's new experience. Then, when the difficulty arises, they can identify the situation and know how to cope with it without letting it rock their understanding or their relationship with God. For example, if we know that a big move is coming up for our family, we can begin to think through the spiritual framework our children will need to help them grow closer in relationship with God through the big move. Here are a couple of possibilities:

- Read some scripture yourself and reflect on Bible stories of where people moved and God was with them: Abram followed God's directions to move to the land that would become Israel; Priscilla and Aquila were forced to move out of their home unexpectedly and had to choose another town to live in; the Israelites were desperate to leave Egypt, but they often felt terrified and insecure in their journey to a new land. Once you have finished reading, you can create windows into how you processed the stories. You can also invite your teens to comment on what you are learning.

- Create opportunities to hear people's stories of how they processed who God was and what he did when they moved. You might invite those friends over for dinner or ask them out after church. Ask them hypothetical questions to get the conversation moving: 'Do you think God already has lined up friends for us in the new place, or do you think that responsibility is totally on our shoulders? Why?'

When we can see a new experience in our future, we can address our teen's questions ahead of time. That way when they experience it, they already have a framework for understanding who God is and how they can engage with him in it.

It's not about being right, but about showing them how to find the next step

Life with God can be complex and full of and ups and downs. We need not feel the pressure to explain things perfectly or to present ideas in just the right way or to be our teen's resident super-theologian. We are placed in our teens' lives not to be their search engine or their always-ready-with-a-right-answer machine.

We are here to be a human, on a journey with God, walking alongside our teenagers and helping them find their own path. We can help tie together truth and experience for them so they can learn how faith and God are woven into all of life. Our goal is to explain what we can, help them walk a tied-together life, and show them how they can continue to walk forward when they have questions. Your journey, just as it is, is a valuable gift to your teenagers.

> We are placed in our teens' lives not to be their search engine or their always-ready-with-a-right-answer machine.

_ 4 _

CONVERSATIONAL PRAYER: CHAT

The basis for much of our emotional connection with family and friends comes from all the verbal and non-verbal communication that freely flows between us. Our relationships are full of laughter and hanging out, doing routine chores together and singing along to music, being near during stressful and confusing times. Our relationships are full of non-verbal signals: smiles, eyebrow movements, head wiggles, shrugs and tears. From the comfortable companionship of being quiet in a car to the heart-to-heart conversations we have in surprising moments, experiencing life together builds affection and trust day by day.

We want our children to have that kind of depth, trust, joy and freedom in their relationships with God, too. Often, however, our teenagers come to view their communication with God – their prayers – as just a method for leaving messages on God's voicemail hoping he will pick up and do something with them. Prayer can become, at worst, an obligation or, at best, a performance that can hopefully draw God's attention and spur him into action.

Often the formulas for prayer that we give our children unintentionally create a rigid box that they can feel trapped in. Teens become hindered by the 'right' way to pray: what their body is supposed to be doing or what words they're supposed to say and the order in which they should say them. The details get all wrapped up in their head and they stop wanting to pray. As a result, they are not drawn into an actual connection with God because they struggle to find their authentic voice in talking with him.

We can remove those hindrances from our teenagers so they can get out of their heads, out of performance mode, out of worrying about whether or not they're saying the right thing, and just feel free to express themselves to God.

One of the reasons Jesus came to earth, died and rose again was to offer us – including our teenagers – the gift of a genuine relationship with God filled with communication flowing freely back and forth. After all, he is the God who can understand, love, listen to and guide us; he is the God who can lead us into all truth, show us the lies of the world, walk alongside us in our choices and give us freedom from sin and shame when we go astray.

Our role as parents is to help our teens become confident in *their own way* of freely communicating with God, sharing their life with him and knowing what God is communicating back to them.

In this chapter, we will look at how our teenagers can feel free to chat to God, and in the next chapter we will look at how God chats back to them.

Chatting to God

Often teenagers first learn how to talk to God while praying in a group at church or at home. For instance, we may pray together at mealtimes for our food or in the morning for a good day at school. Our prayers together may focus on group requests or may feel tokenistic at times. Overall, the topics aren't as deep or as varied as the ones in our private prayers. Rarely do our teens hear the genuine, personal way individuals pray when they are alone with God, so they can be surprised when we encourage them to chat to God in a way that is genuine and intimate.

Our teens may not know that in scripture there are many examples of authentic, intimate prayer. The Psalms are full of people of all ages, from a teenage shepherd to elderly leaders of national worship, communicating with God using astonishingly raw language. The writers seem to hold nothing back from passionate worship: 'As a deer thirsts for streams of water, so I thirst for you, God' (Psalm 42:1, NCV). They express their anguish of feeling disconnected from God: 'How long will you forget me, Lord? Forever? How long will you hide from me?… Lord, look at me. Answer me, my God; tell me, or I will die' (Psalm 13: 1, 3, NCV). They throw open their hearts to God and invite him in: 'Lord, tell me your ways. Show me how to live. Guide me in your truth, and teach me, my God, my Saviour. I trust you all day long' (Psalm 25:4–5, NCV). They let out their rage and anger about the people who hurt them: 'Let death take away my enemies. Let them die while they are still young because evil lives with them' (Psalm 55:15, NCV).

Our prayers may look like that, too. We talk to God about personal struggles, our marriage relationships, parenting woes and the bizarrely aggressive boss we have at work. We talk about our private doubts and the things that make us feel insecure. Within the secret places of our hearts, we put everything on the table before God and talk to him about all of it.

Our teenagers also experience many big emotions. Their lives at school and with their friends are complex, and they feel overwhelmed at times. If they add in puberty, social media and higher consequences for mistakes, teens are aware they need a God who can help them with all of that, but they just don't know how to talk to him.

In Matthew 6, when Jesus was teaching on a hillside, he talked to the crowd about how to pray. He described how some people pray in front of others to get attention and others pray in a certain way to try to impress God with their fancy words. But Jesus assured his followers that secret, private, authentic prayers are the ones God values. He encouraged them to pray about the ordinary things of their lives, the food they need, the struggles and sins of the day, the help they need in the moment.

Teens need to know that God wants to hear their authentic, unfiltered, ordinary thoughts and worries about their day. They don't have to perform for him or pray in any particular way. There is no right way to share their heart with him. They can simply chat about anything on their heart: the big stuff, the small stuff, the important and the ordinary.

Teens need to know that God wants to hear their authentic, unfiltered, ordinary thoughts.

Since prayer is simply communicating with God, then how the disciples lived with Jesus, God on earth, is a model of prayer for us. The disciples weren't walking along the road and saying, 'Dear Jesus, please pass the bread. Amen.' They laughed with him and talked with him. They told him about their hopes and dreams and asked him questions. I'm sure they even played road-trip games on their long walks. They shared their daily life with Jesus. And our teenagers can do that too.

Our goal is to shift our teens from seeing prayer as a performance or a duty, to the idea that prayer is sharing their thoughts and emotions with God as they happen. When teenagers understand this, it can change how they approach a relationship with God.

One teenage boy I know began to have lunches with God at school. Occasionally his friendship group was too much for him when the politics and drama were high. During those times he would just say to himself, 'I need a God-and-me lunch', and he would head off into the field at school and spend time chatting with God about anything he wanted. He told me he always felt lighter after his lunches with God.

Another teenage boy wasn't much of a talker. He told me, 'When I feel full of my emotions, I just take the dog and I go on a walk with God. God puts his hand on my back and we just walk. I just sort of ask God to read my mind because I don't know how to say what's inside. I just take deep breaths, and we just walk.'

One teenage girl told me when she lies in bed at night, she replays memories of her day for God and tells him what she thinks about each memory.

Another teenager loved writing, so he took all of his emotions and wrote them into poems to God, each of them his personal version of a psalm. They were raw and genuine and carried him through some rough times.

Every teen will share their thoughts and emotions with God differently. They will find their own unique way of communicating with him and sharing their life with him. So how do we as parents help them find that freedom in prayer? We can:

- create windows into our authentic prayers
- wade into ideas about prayer
- create opportunities for them to try it themselves.

Create windows

As our teens become comfortable with the idea that chatting to God can be personal, authentic and genuine, they will need glimpses into what that looks like in others' lives. The primary way our teens will see this is if we occasionally let our own internal prayers come out of our mouths. We don't need to start praying aloud all the time, but once in a while, when your teen may overhear, pray out loud. While you are cooking or doing DIY, start chatting aloud to God about how you feel about a situation or your family. Pray for whatever you want; just let it come out of your mouth so that your teens can overhear you connecting with God and can learn how to do it and how normal and natural it is. If you're in the car and happen to pass an accident, let that kneejerk prayer – 'Oh God, keep us safe and heal those people' – slip out of your mouth rather than stay in your thoughts. Create windows into how your informal chatting with God works.

Wade into ideas about prayer – framing

Teenagers sometimes have so many preconceptions or baggage around the idea of prayer that I find it helpful to stop calling it *prayer*. I tend to frame it as *chatting with God*, as that implies an informal, relational, two-way conversation, rather than any particular set of expectations they may have in their head. If you notice your teen struggling with the idea of prayer, it may be helpful to swap out the word. 'Have you chatted with God about it?' sounds much more doable to a teen than 'Have you included it in your prayers?' The first sounds like you are asking about a relationship, while the second sounds like you are asking if they did a task. Framing prayer as something natural they already know how to do can help demystify the idea for teens.

Teenagers also need help understanding when, where and how *chatting with God* can happen. Put a frame around the parts of your day that include when you prayed informally, and tell the brief story without making prayer the central part: 'I was walking to the shops and telling God about this new project I'm working on. Have I told you about my new project? It's exciting.' You can tell stories of when you were angry and you told God about it, or when you were bored and talked to God and how grateful you were that he never gets bored listening to you. Most children are shocked to discover that we chat with God while driving, working or cooking. I take God out to dinner and a movie sometimes and chat with him through the whole thing. During our first lockdown in the Covid-19 pandemic, I told my family how I loved going into the bathroom and sitting on the side of the bath with God, not talking to him at all. God knew I was an introvert and that I didn't want to talk anymore. I just wanted to sit quietly with someone who didn't need anything from me – and that was God. Share with your children when, where and how you chat with God. It will free them to find their own times with him too.

Teenagers need us to help them broaden their understanding of prayer. We can do this by casually adding new ideas to their understanding from time to time. Maybe you can mention you were reading this book and were intrigued with the idea that prayer is about sharing life with God as the disciples did. Maybe you are someone who values set prayers in your personal connection to God. If so, you can mention *how* those written words are a genuine and authentic way of giving voice to your emotions as you pray. Teens may need to hear other people's experiences, too, of *how* they primarily chat with God through art or by going for a walk or writing in a journal. The more we can enable our teens to be surrounded by people who openly discuss how they authentically connect with God, the more they can feel comfortable and confident in exploring what that looks like for them.

Create opportunities

Alongside conversations about prayer, our teens need opportunities to experience it. Some parents create comfortable opportunities at home rather than using the traditional 'everyone out loud and in order around the circle' way to pray. This could mean giving everyone five minutes to respond personally to a Bible reading by drawing, writing, lying on the sofa and talking to God in their head, or any other way they choose.

Some parents invite their teens to join them whenever they themselves have time with God. One mum's main connection time with God was when she jogged, so she extended an invitation to her teens to join her on her run with God any time they wanted. One day her middle child showed up, ready to jog. 'How does this work?' the daughter asked. The mum said, 'I just run and chat to God, and I stay ready for when he chats back. Feel free to do the same. If you want to talk about it after we run, I'd love to hear about it, but otherwise, I respect that your time with God is between you two.' Over the next four years, her teenagers joined, dropped out and joined again. They all told me how significant that time was and how it helped them establish their own patterns with God. One daughter still runs with God at uni, but the others found different ways that worked better for them. One likes to curl up on a couch and journal, and the other likes to read over breakfast and chat to God on his bus ride. Once the mum created space for her teens to experience her way of connecting with God, her teens became inspired to go on their own journey of finding a pattern that works best for them.

It is not about you

At this point, some of us may be thinking, *I'm not in a good place with God right now*, or, *I'm still at the beginning of all this prayer stuff myself. I don't think creating windows into my prayer life will be the best example for my teens.*

It's okay. You may want to tell your teens, 'I've been trying to pray differently recently and I'm not sure how I feel about it,' and then share your experiences. You may end up giving voice to their experiences as well. Your windows may be about trying a new way of chatting to God or laughing at trying something that didn't work. In either case, you will be modelling for your teens that finding your voice and pattern of connection with God is a journey. What works today may not work tomorrow, so we readjust and reassess how we connect with God.

If you are in a season of struggling, it is okay to create a window into that, too, with wisdom. It is okay to say, 'I think I fell out of my pattern of connecting with God, and that's been hard for me. I'm not giving up, though. I'm trying new things. Any

If you are in a season of struggling, it is okay to create a window into that, too, with wisdom.

ideas?' Again, what you are modelling for your teen is that struggling isn't the end, that wrestling isn't the signal to walk away. It's just an invitation to adjust.

God never designed us to parent alone. We are surrounded by friends, church family and the broader experience of other Christians around the world. Invite other people to share their stories with you and your family. Mention posts on social media that intrigue you or apps you find useful. Tell stories you hear from others.

Every season and stage that you are in is valuable to your teenager because at some point, they will find themselves in a similar situation, and they will have your example of what to do when they are there. Your imperfect journey with God is a gift to your teens because it makes them feel normal and free to be themselves.

When we remind our teenagers that God values, understands and loves hearing all of their messy, authentic thoughts and emotions, we can free our children to find their own voices with God. What more could we want than our teenagers wholeheartedly sharing their lives with the God who loves them?

The beautiful thing about God is that chatting with him is more than just sharing ourselves with him. It's also about God responding *to* us. In the next chapter, we will talk about how we can help our teenagers catch God's communications to them.

- 5 -

CONVERSATIONAL PRAYER: CATCH

I met Jordan at a summer camp a few years ago when he signed up to be a teenage leader with my team. A few days later we were chatting after a session, and he told me about his life. Jordan had been with a foster family for two years, and he was beginning to feel nervous about leaving care because of his age. He radiated anxiety and fear. There was nothing I could say to make his situation better, and I had no authority or influence to assure him of what might happen.

'What has God been saying to you about it?' I asked.

Jordan shrugged. 'I pray about it, but my social worker hasn't told me for sure what will happen.'

I realised Jordan only expected God to respond by either doing what he asked or not doing what he asked. That was it. I smiled a bit. 'Jordan, God wants to chat to us as much as we chat to him. He has all sorts of help for us. He promises to guide us into truth, lead us to know what to do next and share what he is thinking and feeling with us. I wonder what he might want to say to you about this situation. Do you want to ask him?'

Jordan's eyes widened. 'Yes!' he said.

I quickly shared the different ways God can communicate with him and encouraged him to chat to God and wait for God to respond. I told him that I would be hanging around for a while if he wanted to talk about his experience when he was done.

Jordan found some space by himself to pray while I continued cleaning up. Every once in a while, I would glance over and see him with his head in his hands, sitting cross-legged against the back wall. After ten minutes, I saw him stand up. His face was a bit swollen and covered with tears. As he walked over to me, a big smile began to spread across his face.

'How do you feel?' I asked.

'Like I can breathe again,' he said, and sighed.

'What was God doing with you?'

Jordan glanced back at the wall. 'I was just sitting there telling God all about how stressed and worried I was and how I felt like everything around me was knocking me side to side. Then a picture popped in my head of a big old pirate ship in a storm. The waves were huge and crashing on top of it, and it was almost getting tipped over by the wind and waves. The storm was pushing the ship closer and closer to some big sharp rocks, and if it hit the rocks, it would crash and sink. I was like, "That is exactly how I feel!"'

He choked up for a second, then continued: 'When I get out of care, I'm afraid I'm going to crash and there is no way to avoid it. Then in my head, the ship dropped this big anchor thing with a huge chain, and even though the storm kept going, the ship stopped getting pushed to the rocks. It stayed safe, even though it was still getting tossed around. I just got a really strong feeling that God was saying he was my anchor and I didn't need to be worried about the storm. I just needed to hang on to my anchor and I wouldn't crash. Then the storm stopped and the ship was okay. And around the ship, there were loads of other boats.'

His voice choked up again: 'The big waves hid the other boats, but they were there the whole time. Like I won't be alone when it's time to go. Like God will give me other boats around me. That was my biggest fear – that I would be alone. But I just need to hold on to God, not let the storm scare me and know that God will bring me people when I need them. And my anchor will go with me.'

In any relationship, communication must flow both ways. Very few of us would stay in a relationship if we were the only one communicating. It's no fun chatting with someone unless the other person chats back! God is faithful to communicate with us in various ways, and we can train and equip our teenagers to seek, expect and know God's voice in their daily lives. When they can access his voice, they can access *him*: his truth, love, healing, encouragement, holiness, challenges, peace and so much more.

The Bible is full of God's promises that we will hear and know his voice. He promises he will speak to us when we call to him, and at times he will even initiate those conversations with us. Many people in the Bible experienced God initiating a conversation with them: Abram, Moses, Samuel, Gideon, Mary, the Samaritan woman at the well, Zacchaeus. God's communication is not meant to be a once-in-a-lifetime occurrence, but part of our daily, ordinary relationship with him because he *wants* to communicate with us (John 16:12–15).

Jesus described himself as a shepherd whose sheep hear and know his voice. He promises that we will grow to recognise his voice so well that we will run away from other voices that try to guide or influence us:

> The one who enters by the gate is the shepherd of the sheep. The gatekeeper opens the gate for him, and the sheep listen to his voice. He calls his own sheep by name and leads them out. When he has brought out all his own, he goes on ahead of them,

and his sheep follow him because they know his voice. But they will never follow a stranger; in fact, they will run away from him because they do not recognise a stranger's voice.

JOHN 10:2–5 (NIV)

For me, the key word in this Bible passage is 'recognise'. Recognition is a process involving experience over time. If someone you have known for a long time, such as a family member or friend, called you from an unknown number, they would only need to say, 'Hey, it's me', and you would know who it is. You have heard their voice so many times you would instantly recognise the tone and pitch.

God wants our teenagers to become so familiar with his voice that they instantly recognise his truth, guidance, love and comfort. But that kind of recognition will take time to develop. We can help our teens on their journey of learning to recognise God's voice – his communication – in their daily lives and accompany them as they grow in confidence to respond to what he is saying to them.

So how can we help our teenagers have vibrant, two-way communications with God? We can:

- prepare our children for the ways God speaks
- create windows in our lives to help them see what it might look like for them
- wade into ideas that will help them understand and feel confident
- create opportunities for them to grow in experience with God.

Prepare children for the ways God speaks

When we are new to the idea of God speaking to us, we tend to have narrow expectations of what that experience should be like. For example, I was convinced that if God were to communicate with me, he would sound like a Shakespearean actor with a booming posh voice. I know other people who expected God's communication to be an elusive whisper, so they felt it was necessary to listen carefully in complete silence. The problem is that when we become focused on what the experience *should be* like, we can miss out on what God's communications *actually are* like.

When it comes to perceiving God's communication to us, I often use the word 'catching', as it helps us picture the approach we need. 'Listening' implies the process is audial, so we can become fixated on 'hearing' God's voice with our ears. 'Catching', on the other hand, implies a readiness and awareness to receive what God communicates no matter how he chooses to do so.

God created us for a relationship with him, so our *bodies* are designed to facilitate that. God is not limited by words; he communicates in various ways that we can catch with our whole being. All we need to do is *be ready* to catch. God's messages can pass by us unnoticed if we're not aware he's communicating with us. We may be so focused on expecting him to speak in one way that we forget to keep ready all the other ways we can catch his communication.

Teenagers need us to talk with them about how God communicates. Too often, our teenagers are surrounded with only vague ideas of what it looks like and feels like to have God communicate with us. They may hear adults around them say things like, 'I just felt led by God to…', or, 'I had a sense that God might be pointing me to…' Teenagers need to know not only that we thought God was communicating, but also *how* we came to that conclusion and *how* we recognised that it was God. If we are to help our teens truly be open to what God is communicating to them and to give them encouragement on their journey of recognising it, we need to be willing to equip them with specifics in knowing how to catch what he is saying.

Here are several main ways we can catch what God is saying to us. Don't feel you need to be an expert at perceiving God's voice. We *all* are on a lifelong journey of learning how to recognise his voice in our lives. You may be at the beginning of this journey yourself, or you may feel very comfortable perceiving what God is saying to you. Wherever you are, let's remind ourselves of the different ways we see God speak in scripture and in our lives. Which ways do you experience most often in your own life?

With our brain (Acts 2:17–18; 9:10; Joel 2:28)

Pictures or movies in our mind

Take one second to close your eyes and picture your family. You don't see them with your eyes, but you can picture them in your mind. That same place of picturing is a prime area of communication for God. We can use it to show God pictures of how we feel, our memories or hopes, or what has happened in our day. He also loves dropping into that place pictures of his own he wants to show us, movies of how he sees things, and his hopes and dreams and suggestions for us.

Like Jordan's experience in our opening story, pictures can be a wonderful means of communication between God and us. Teenagers can be quite visual and creative, and God often meets with them in this way. Some teens like using a journal or sketchbook to capture their pictures from God to look back on or discuss with us later if they want.

Teenagers can be quite visual and creative, and God often meets with them in this way

Words in our mind

If we can sing in our heads or read a book silently, we can identify that place in our mind where we use words and 'hear' things without using our ears. We often chat to God by speaking only inside our heads, and he can chat back to us in that same place. Some teenagers have entire conversations with God this way, while others pick up only words or phrases from him. God can remind teenagers of Bible verses they have heard or learned in the past, or he can give them a

Bible verse reference to look up so he can continue to speak to them through his word.

One teen I worked with struggled with exams due to his severe dyslexia and anxiety. He told me that one day he became aware of God sitting with him in an exam. On that day his anxiety was climbing, and his negative thoughts were running on a constant loop. Then suddenly, a soft thought interrupted his anxious mind: *My peace I give to you*. The teen told me he instantly recognised God was with him because he remembered that Jesus said those words in the Bible to his followers. He quickly chatted to God about his feelings, and he felt the same voice in his mind assure him, *I am with you; you are not alone*. The young man told me that from then on whenever he went into an exam, he felt as if God was with him just like God was with David on the battlefield with Goliath.

Guided thoughts
Sometimes, when we think deeply about something, solutions pop into our mind or we arrive at a place where we feel good about our decision. God loves helping us think about big questions and he participates in our thinking process.

When I was in Switzerland with a group of teens, our group spent some free time outdoors with God. The teens went all over the hillside writing, drawing, swinging, reading and doing whatever best enabled them to connect with God. I noticed that one girl kept staring at a facing hill with fierce determination, so I walked over to see how she was doing. She told me, 'God's been showing me those two trees over there and telling me how we are like them. God is planted next to me, and our roots are all grown together. He'll stand next to me through all of my life.' God was guiding her thoughts and speaking to her about trees planted many years ago. The idea of being rooted with God reminded her of something she read in the Bible once, so later she went back to her Bible and investigated it further.

With our skin (1 Kings 8:10–11)

Some people perceive God with their bodies, by having a physical sense of God's closeness. They sometimes experience tingles, a warmth, a heavy head or a sensation they can't explain. One teenager with a chronic condition told me that almost every time when she was in recovery after surgery, she felt a warmth in one of her hands as if someone was holding her hand, and she knew it was God.

With our emotions (John 14:27; Philippians 4:7; 1 Peter 1:8–9)

God created emotions, and we can catch these from him if we are willing. Many teenagers become so focused on 'listening' for God's responses that they entirely miss the deep sense of peace God gives them as they talk with him. When we describe to our teens that we can catch God's emotions – his peace, excitement, joy and sense of justice, for instance – they recognise how often God has been communicating with them through feelings or emotions.

A teenager told me a story of a time when he was struggling during lockdown in the Covid-19 pandemic. He felt lonely, and he was angry with his family for intruding into his space, with school for all the homework and with his friends for abandoning him. He was telling God about it, and then he felt an unexplainable weight lift off him. He said it was as if a light turned on inside him and he could smile again. He felt as if God gave him some of his joy because he, the teen, couldn't find any himself. Whenever he felt that cloud of stress coming back on him, he would ask God for his light and joy to help him out of it again.

With our ears and eyes (2 Kings 6:10–17; Acts 7:54–56)

Some people hear God's voice audibly or see things that only they can see. It can be a powerful way of perceiving God. One day a tween boy on one of my children's ministry teams said that he never got words or pictures in his mind from God, but when he chatted with God, he felt as if God's voice was so clear that he could hear it with his ears.

With our guts (1 Corinthians 12:8; John 4:1–9)

This is the indescribable feeling of surety that you know something. Sometimes teens can feel the rightness or wrongness of a situation or an instinct that they can't logically explain. Teens have often told me they've been at a party and something 'just didn't feel right'. They felt God told them to leave, so they did. Sometimes teens have seen someone being cruel to another teen at school and they felt convinced that God wanted them to do something about it. Telling our teens about this way of catching God's communication can encourage them to pay attention to that prompting that doesn't come in words but is recognisable anyway.

A teenage girl told me about a time at school when she was leaving the toilets but felt something was wrong. She couldn't explain what it was. She just had a gut feeling that she should go back into the toilets. When she did, she heard crying in one of the stalls, and she asked the girl who was inside if she was okay. After some talking, she discovered that the crying girl was considering suicide. The teen was able to help this girl connect with the adults at school who gave her the support she needed.

In dreams (Genesis 20:3; Matthew 2:13; Job 33:14–18)

God speaks in dreams, and our teenagers can catch some great communication from God while they sleep. Not every dream is from God, but every once in a while teens may get a sense that maybe God was trying to tell them something in a dream. Some teens keep a notebook next to their bed so they can write down any dreams they feel are important to pray about or discuss with us later.

One of the older youth I worked with told me about a dream he had when he was applying for university. At the time he was apprehensive his grades wouldn't be good enough to get in. One night he dreamed of slowly sinking in mud, and no matter how much he struggled, he couldn't get out. Then Jesus came towards him, walking on the top of the mud, and pulled him out and told him, 'Just keep your eyes on me.' He woke up free from worry, confident that whatever would happen was going to be okay because Jesus would guide him.

* * *

God speaks to us in many wonderful ways. As individuals, we are each catching from God in ways that are unique and authentic to us. Eventually, we develop our own patterns of how and when we catch God's communications best. Some teenagers connect with God best outside in nature as God guides their thoughts of him; others love a quiet room and solitude as God shows them Bible verses; others paint conversations with him in pictures. While it is good to encourage teens to develop their preferences, it is also vital that we keep highlighting the need to stay open to every way of perceiving God's voice, so our teens don't miss anything he is saying to them.

Creating windows

Teens often see things in extremes – can or can't, now or never – and they may approach their relationship with God in the same way. When we create windows into our own learning process of recognising God's communications in our lives, our teens can see how our understanding of his voice slowly builds up over time. In fact, we will be in the middle of this learning process for the rest of our lives!

If you are new to this idea of conversational prayer with God or catching his communications, it's fantastic to share that with your teens too. Sometimes the best journey you can show your teens is when you are trying something new. You can say you've been reading a book about some of the different ways God communicates and you want to be more aware of God's voice in your life. Share your stories of how it's going and what is working. Talk about the disappointing time you went for a walk to see if being out in nature was where you could best perceive God's communications, but instead you just wandered around cold and grumpy. Share about how you were reading the Bible and a story filled you with enormous peace about a situation in your life. When we show our teens that going on a journey of being open to God's communications is imperfect and messy and worth the process of trying, we give them the courage to try it themselves.

Feel free to create strategic windows into how God's communications are personally helping you in the moment. If you keep a journal, you can show your children a page or two of the pictures God dropped in your mind or the truths he is challenging you about. Talk about how God's voice has helped shape your decisions or influenced the way you feel about current situations. Take Bible verses God used to encourage you and stick them on your mirror so your teenagers can see how you use scripture to remind yourself of his truth. Create windows so your teens can see that sometimes God communicates with us for the purpose of impacting others.

One dad I know had a friend from childhood who was having health struggles and didn't know God. While on the bus with his children, the dad mentioned that when he was chatting with God about his friend, God reminded him of a childhood memory from 15 years ago. He said the memory played in his head like a little movie of when his terrified friend had to go into hospital. The dad shared his plan to bring up that memory with his friend the next time he saw him, because the dad felt God reminded him of it for a reason. Weeks later, he gave his teens an update and said that when he shared the memory with his friend, his friend talked honestly about his current health fears, and then he got to pray with his friend for the first time in their long friendship. A few weeks later over breakfast, the father shared he had a gut feeling he needed to message his friend an encouragement that God hadn't forgotten him, so he sent the message right away. The teen children were with their dad when the friend messaged back and said he had been praying for the first time and the dad's text was exactly what he was praying about. Each time the dad opened a window for his teens to see him catch God's communications and follow through with what God impressed him to do, the teens learned more of how God communicates in different yet distinct ways to serve his purposes in our lives and in others' lives too.

Wade into ideas

One of the most important truths we can equip our teenagers with is how to tell the difference between authentic communications from God and their own imaginations. We don't want our teenagers running around thinking every thought that pops into their heads is from God. The worry that our teens may get confused about whether or not a particular communication is from God can make some of us shy away altogether from the idea of catching God's communications. I completely understand the worry; however, I am *not* worried that teens will be confused at times and make mistakes in learning how to perceive God's communication. They will.

Everything your teen has ever learned has been through a process of trial and error, mistakes and corrections. When our children were tiny, we understood their learning process would be messy. We cheered them on as they learned to walk. We applauded their efforts as they took their first steps, and we laughed or comforted them when they fell. Even now they're still learning to dress themselves well, build friendships, cook and be responsible, all through the same process of acquiring new information and applying it to new situations by trial and error, mistakes and corrections. And as parents, we still encourage them to keep trying, and we applaud and celebrate their progress.

> Everything your teen has ever learned has been through a process of trial and error, mistakes and corrections.

As our teenagers try to recognise God's voice in their lives, their learning process will be just as messy as it is for any other new skill, and we can respond to their efforts with the same encouragement and celebration as we always do. We need to remind ourselves this is a learning *process*. More important, our teens need to know it is a process, too.

Everyone on this journey learns to 'discern' God's voice by taking what they perceive to be from God and checking it against some key measurements:

- Does it sound like God?
- What is the fruit of that communication?
- What do wise people think?

Your senior leaders at your church go through this discernment process. You go through this process. And your teens can go through this process too.

Does it sound like God?

Teenagers need to be taught how to assess whether what they perceive matches with what we know about God from the Bible.

Teenagers understand this idea quickly. If you had a firm rule that your teen wasn't allowed to watch 18-rated movies, and you've been passionate and adamant about this their whole life, they would not doubt your position. If their friend then said to them, 'Oh, by the way, your mum said it was okay if we watch this 18-rated movie at my house,' your teen wouldn't believe it. Your teen *knows* you, knows what you stand for and knows you would never say anything like that. Instantly your teen would conclude their friend was lying. Whatever our teenagers hear or perceive as from God must be held up to that same sort of unwavering, absolute standard.

Assessing the truth is easier for our teens when they are both God-smart and God-connected! For example, if your teenager is chatting with God after feeling he failed his GCSE mock exams, and he thinks God is telling him to drop out of school because he is stupid and worthless, then you can help him assess whether that is from God or is a lie. Hold up that experience to God's character and his word and say, 'Would the God we know in our lives and see in the Bible ever call you worthless?' Hear what your teen has to say, comfort him in the process, have a look at the Bible if you want and help him take the next step of what to do with those thoughts that aren't from God.

We must not only help children to discern God's voice, but also teach them what to do with thoughts that aren't from him. Any teenager's thoughts that are potentially damaging to themselves or others *do not get to stay in their heads*. I explain to teenagers that they can put those negative words or pictures in a box in their head and shrink it until the box disappears, because God does not want us to let those thoughts poison our hearts and minds (see e.g. Philippians 4:8; 2 Corinthians 10:5). Some teenagers can struggle with negative thoughts, and this is an excellent opportunity to help them develop skills to cope with them.

What is the fruit?

God wants to encourage us, give us hope, draw us close to him and take us on a journey of becoming more like him. If what we perceive as from God makes us want to distance ourselves from him, it probably wasn't from God. Even when God convicts us of sin, he does it to show us his grace and to invite us to put aside what is holding us back from him. I tell teenagers that if they feel afraid or want to run away from God, their experience probably wasn't from God and they can put it out of their heads. God's communication will always draw us closer to him.

What do wise people think?

God has put us in a community with people who also are connected to God, so if we aren't sure what God is communicating to us, we can write it down and talk with others about it. Sometimes people can help, but other times they can be wrong and unhelpful. It is still up to *us* to decide what God is saying to us. We can always ask God to help us understand, because he is the one who made us and knows best how to communicate his own voice to our hearts and minds.

Our teens need to know that sometimes we chat with others about what we think God is communicating to us. I sometimes show teens my personal journal where I write down communications I think are from God and put big question marks next to things I'm still weighing and deciding if they're from him. You could mention to your teen how you were wondering with your friend about something you thought God dropped in your mind. You could let your teens know that if they want to, they could do some wondering with you about what God may be saying to them, too.

Creating new opportunities to connect with God

Teenagers benefit from having safe times and places to explore the idea that God communicates with them. When we help our teens dip their toes in the water of catching from God, they can begin to feel a bit more confident to try it on their own.

Try setting aside moments of space for your family to invite in God's communications. If you are a family who prays before a meal, try adding a bit of space at the end of the prayer before moving on. Rather than say just a quick 'Thank you, God, for this food, and bless the hands who made it. Amen,' tell your family you'd like to try something a bit different and explain what you want to do. For instance, say you noticed you were just talking at God during the meal prayer and not allowing him space to respond. You would like to ask God something at the end of the prayer, and then give everyone a few seconds to catch from God or wait in silence until you say, 'Amen'. Then simply do your regular pattern but add a little invitation at the end like this:

'Thank you, God, for this food, and bless the hands that made it. Help us know you are here with us now.' Then wait quietly for ten seconds to allow everyone to have a few moments to be aware of God. Finish with: 'Thank you that you are here with us. Amen.'

Don't feel tied to the words I just suggested. You could invite God to do anything – bring his peace, remind us of a time he was with us today, whatever you want. By expecting God to respond and creating space for him to do so, you raise the expectation that he will, and you show your teens that even ten seconds of space with God is valuable. Whether it's at mealtimes, at bedtimes or before school, add in those little moments and invite God in.

You might also want to create space for God within the places you go. For instance, if you have a creative teen, let them bring a sketchpad to church so they can draw while they listen and create a visual of what they feel God may be communicating to them or what point from the talk sticks in their head. I know many teens who can catch from God clearer as they let their hands doodle on the paper. You are the expert in your teenagers. In whatever ways you feel are right, create space for your teens and your family to explore catching from God.

It's not all down to you

God has placed your family in a wider community so you would not be alone in helping your teen on this beautiful journey of catching God's communications. As you create windows into your journey, remember to invite others from your church community to share with you and your family their experiences of hearing God's voice, too. We are all on this same journey of learning to recognise his voice in our lives. As parents, we can equip, encourage and support our teenagers as they learn how to establish a life of conversation with God.

– 6 –

UNWINDING WARPED VIEWS OF GOD

Working with children isn't usually glamorous, but when I received an invitation to work with young teens at a camp in the Alps, I quickly agreed. Images of myself spinning in ankle-deep grass singing 'The hills are alive' like Maria von Trapp flooded my mind. I pictured a group of young teens, all in matching outfits, laughing and obediently following me around while I helped them discover a deep connection with God, not music. It was going to be perfect.

Unfortunately, rather than running into a replica of *The Sound of Music*, I discovered something surprising: even though the young teens were all Christians, they seemed utterly uninterested in connecting with God. No matter how much I taught about connecting with him through prayer or music or how many personal stories I told, the young people still seemed resistant to engage.

My curiosity got the better of me, so I threw out the next session's teaching and went on an exploration. I asked the teenagers to describe God to me, and they effortlessly began to rattle off a list of words: loving, kind, gracious, always there, knows everything. On and on they went until my flip-chart sheet was full. They knew all the right answers, yet their knowledge of God's character didn't make an ounce of difference to their connection with him.

I started a fresh sheet of flip-chart paper. 'You have done a great job of telling me what the Bible says about God,' I said. 'But I would like you to tell me what it genuinely feels like to have God in your life. Please describe to me your experience of who God is to you. Describe to me the God you know.'

The teenagers looked at me nervously. No one spoke. 'You won't be in trouble. I honestly want to know,' I assured them. Slowly the flip chart filled up with a completely different list. They felt that God was powerless, uninterested, changeable, uncaring, far away, grumpy. I realised that their problem with connecting with God wasn't because they didn't know how; it was because they didn't want to. Sometimes we can forget that for our children to connect with God, for teens to build a relationship with him, they first have to like him and see him for who he really is.

Jesus certainly believed that how we viewed God was important. Part of why he came to earth was to enable us to see past religious rules and behaviour, past experience and confusion, past our own misconceptions and understand who God really is. One day when Jesus was discussing with his disciples about life after death, they wanted to know more about the character and nature of God:

> Philip said to him, 'Lord, show us the Father. That is all we need.' Jesus answered, 'I have been with you a long time now. Do you still not know me, Philip? Whoever has seen me has seen the Father. So why do you say, "Show us the Father"? Don't you believe that I am in the Father and the Father is in me? The words I say to you don't come from me, but the Father lives in me and does his own work.'
> JOHN 14:8–10 (NCV)

Jesus often challenged people's misunderstandings of God and clarified what the Father really wants for us all. He gave people vital knowledge and experience of himself and of the Father, which they could use to weave a more accurate understanding of God.

Weaving an understanding of God

All of us are on a process of weaving together an understanding of who God is. We take the threads of scripture and sermons, books and conversations, and we weave an idea of what God is like. We add in threads of when God is faithful, proves his love to us or provides for our needs. We also weave in our disappointments, confusions and doubts. All these threads woven together make up our view of God, and through them we interact with him and respond to him.

At times we may learn that some of our threads are, in fact, inaccurate or incomplete. We then can learn how to remove those false threads from our view of God and correct our mistakes. Eventually we learn how to wisely assess what threads are useful to weave into our understanding of God, and what threads are untrue or unhelpful and should be discarded *before* we let them impact us.

Our teenagers are inexperienced in assessing the threads they use to weave together their understanding of God. They take all the threads of their life and throw them into their view of God: RE lessons, friends' opinions, their personal experiences, youth group teaching, children's Bible storybooks, parents' stories of life with God, scripture they read, YouTube clips they see and blogs they half-read. All of these get woven into their view of God and, not surprisingly, our teenagers can end up with some warped views of God that drastically impact how they interact with him. As their parents or carers, we can help our teens spot what threads are inaccurate and we can give them the skills to learn how to choose what threads to weave into their view of God going forward. And like Jesus our shepherd, we can do this in gentle, incremental ways.

Common views of God

I live in Yorkshire, so I see a lot of sheep. I once watched a farmer move his sheep from one field to another and was struck by how he did it. He didn't try to force the sheep to walk along a pathway. Instead, with the help of a few farmhands, he waved the herd away from where they weren't supposed to go and opened wide the gates leading to the right direction. Some sheep followed with little effort, but others ran back and forth several times before they found their way to the right gate.

Teenagers are constantly adjusting their views of God with every new bit of information and experience they get. Like the farmer, we don't need to hyper-control those views or try to regulate our teens to a narrow path of thinking. Instead, we can stand back and give them a lot of freedom to discover God for themselves, and when their understanding of God is heading too far in the wrong direction, we can slowly and gently redirect them back to the truth.

To help redirect our teenagers, we need to understand some of the warped views of God they may accidently construct for themselves. Once we begin to spot how they think about God and why they are responding to him in certain ways, we'll be able to help, like the farmer, by gently nudging them in the right direction. Let's look at the most common warped views of God that we see in teenagers today.

Distant, busy God

In this view, God is far away on a cloud somewhere, working hard. He's got the world to run, people to save, babies to form, missionaries to call and decisions to make about where people go after they die. He exists far away in heaven, removed from our ordinary lives on earth.

Teens can feel their insignificance in the face of all God is doing and how far away he is. You may notice them feeling stressed or at a loss for what to pray about, because they don't want to annoy him with the small stuff they want to say.

Detached God

God may seem to be mysterious and self-focused. He will do what he wants, when he wants and nothing we can say or do will affect him. He is in control, and it's our job to accept that.

At first, teens may angrily struggle with this God, but eventually they'll accept defeat and dismiss him altogether. They believe most circumstances around them, good or bad, happen because of God, so they don't know how to feel about him. They know they are victims to his whims and feel under pressure from adults to accept their fate without resisting.

Super-nice, super-passive, jolly God

This version of God smiles through whatever happens. He sits back and enjoys the worship we send him and has a cliché response to everything. He's happy, and he wants us to be happy no matter what.

Some teens try to charm this God with their good behaviour, hoping to be rewarded. They can feel betrayed when bad things happen, because they think they have earned good things from God and he isn't living up to their imagined deal. Other teens can be dismissive and resentful of this God. They don't want to perform for a God who demands happiness from them, particularly when their reality is full of hardship and difficulty.

Buddy God

This view of God puts the teen at the centre of the relationship – it's all about *me*; I am special, wonderful and loved, and God does everything with me. God is essentially the teen's sidekick, helping them do everything they want to accomplish.

Teens eventually get bored with this God, because he is like their annoying friend who has no personality and follows them around wanting to do whatever they do. This view of God can blind teens to God's power, majesty and purpose, and reduces him to being a tag-along friend.

Indulgent father God

This version of God is the best father a teenager can imagine. He loves them and lavishes them with gifts. He protects them and makes sure nothing negative happens to them or to those they love. He is lenient about sin and waves away their mistakes because he is just so fond of them.

Teens with this view of God feel entitled to good things and feel little conviction for sin, because a loving father wouldn't worry about things like that. When the world seems to not work out the blissful way they expect, they can feel angry at God for not being the father they expected him to be.

Grumpy old grandfather God

This God crosses his arms and complains about kids these days with all their progressive ideas about sexuality, politics and freedom. He disagrees with almost everything the modern world stands for.

Some teens see this version of God as a relic of an ancient time filled with old restrictions, having nothing meaningful to say to the world we live in. Teens can view him as irrelevant to their lives.

Angry God

In this view of God, he sits in the sky on his throne of judgement, critically watching every moment of our day to spot our sins. When he sees one, he flashes his anger and pours out his punishment. He is easily offended and requires everyone around him to be as perfect as possible.

This view of God produces fear in teenagers and often a large cycle of shame. He is impossible to please, so their stress is on doing what God says to avoid his displeasure. Love rarely enters the picture. These teenagers don't seek a relationship with this God, choosing instead either to wrestle with their shame and their fear of punishment or to do the hard work of earning God's forgiveness once again.

Hot and cold God

This God flips back and forth between an indulgent father and an authoritarian and impulsive king, somewhat like Ariel's father, King Triton, in the Disney film *Little Mermaid*.

Sometimes when teens are exposed to contrasting stories in the Bible, they struggle to know how to put them together. God is love, yet he makes war. God is a father, yet he punishes in the Old Testament. This can leave teens walking on eggshells with a potentially explosive God because they aren't sure what mood he will be in or what will cause him to respond in one way or another.

Noticing their views of God and unknotting threads

God has placed us in the everyday lives of our teenagers to help them meet and know him better. One of the beautiful things about being a part of their everyday lives is that we can notice when they are weaving an inaccurate view of God, and then we can help redirect them. The first step we need to take is to uncover what their views of God are. We can do this in several ways.

Ask open-ended questions

Teenagers are in the process of thinking about God and shaping their views of him, but they can be hesitant to talk about it because they know how important their views are to us. Christian teens know the answers they think we want to hear, so if we directly ask them about their views, they are tempted to give us those 'right' answers. So how can we find out our teen's honest views of God when they don't tell us? Ask open-ended questions.

Teenagers need to know it's okay to be wrestling with an idea. They need to know that their doubts and questions are a safe part of exploring who God is and what he does. We can help our teens by normalising the process of pondering an idea, wrestling with it and settling on a view. By doing this, we give our teens the space and confidence to disagree with us. They can be comfortable to explore ideas with us without worrying that we will think they have lost their faith or are no longer convinced that Christianity is true. By encouraging them to talk about their genuine thoughts and showing them that it's okay to wonder about things, we give them the gift of staying on the journey of faith through its ups and downs, not just when it makes complete sense.

To do this, a good place to start is to remove the pressure to have the correct answers, so they can be comfortable talking about God without feeling as if they are being quizzed. We can also shift the way we interact with them about faith by encouraging them to be on their own path of discovering God. One of the most valuable tools I have found for this purpose is to ask questions that don't have right answers.

When we ask questions that don't have right answers, we encourage our teenagers to wonder about God, to apply the knowledge they have of him to hypothetical situations or to sit comfortably without being sure of the answer. Try asking open-ended questions like:

- Do you think Jesus fancied anyone in secondary school?
- The Bible says that God rested after he created everything. Well, I like to watch TV when I rest. What do you think God did?
- Why didn't God just ask somebody else to go to Nineveh when Jonah said no?

We can ask questions that allow our teenagers to say what they think or feel rather than simply reply with the 'right' answer.

One family I know had a 14-year-old daughter who was passionate about science and struggled at school because religion and science felt like opposites. Her faith was wavering because she couldn't see where God and faith fitted into the concrete world of fact and scientific enquiry. Her parents began to increase how much scientific news they commented on at home and how they found it fascinating that God constructed the way the world works, but that wasn't enough. They felt they needed to bring in people who thought like their daughter to help her broaden her view of God in a way that made sense to her. They asked around at church and invited some adults over for dinner who worked in scientific fields, and they asked the scientists pointed questions about their journeys of matching up faith and God with scientific enquiry. The scientists talked about how they saw God in physics and maths and about their journeys of wrestling with ambiguities in scripture. The daughter was able to ask questions, be blunt in her challenges and laugh with others who understood what she was wrestling with. Going forward, the scientists shared books with her, talked over ideas with her after church and gave her names of other people she could talk with about being a Christian and a concrete thinker.

We can also use open-ended questions as we wonder about things we've seen. Maybe you are watching the television series *The Chosen*, about Jesus and his disciples' ministry. As you watch you can wonder out loud, 'Do you think Jesus was like that? I love how funny he is in this programme. Do you think he was that funny in real life?' Or you may come home from a meeting one day and say, 'I have a colleague who was so angry at the injustice of our staff towards our customers that he jumped in and rudely condemned it. It made me think about Jesus flipping over tables or God getting angry with people. Do you think God is okay with rude anger when it's about fairness?' Questions that call our teenagers to process their knowledge of God with the complexities of life will help train them to tie together truth and experience and articulate a view.

Try to hold off on correcting any of your teenager's wayward thinking at that moment, as the most powerful part of this exercise is in releasing them to talk about their real feelings about God. Feel free to share your thoughts at your own wonderings, explore scripture, connect as equals and ponder ideas together. When you do, you will be creating a family culture in which the sharing of genuine thoughts and wonderings is valued above the performance of 'right' answers. Open questions will help you gain insight into your teenager's views of God without needing them to express those views directly.

Notice the clues in their casual communication

Your teen is constantly communicating with you verbally and non-verbally. We often hope they would just come out and clearly say, 'I'm struggling in my faith because, on the one hand, it is something I have known all my life. But, on the other hand, I have prayed and prayed for God's guidance and I have no idea if he even hears me. He hasn't communicated with me, so now I think he either dislikes me or is not real and that is making me feel really annoyed and alone. Therefore, I don't want to go to church and be surrounded by a bunch of people who seem to hear God all the time and will shove it in my face. That's why I'm staying in bed this morning and resisting being ready for church on time.' While a few teens may be this self-aware and verbally communicative, many are not.

Some teens communicate through their behaviour instead. Your teenager may appear to be lazy on a Sunday, dragging their feet while they dress and rolling their eyes at you when you're annoyed with them for making you late to church. Instead of assuming your teen has a self-discipline problem (which may be the case), consider if their behaviour indicates that they are struggling with the idea of God and church.

Some teens communicate by giving opinionated statements. Your teenager may come home from school and announce that Jesus was not a historical figure because their friend at school read an article about it, and so Christianity was just a religion made by a few radicals trying to upend the Jewish population. While your mouth is open in shock at all the things wrong with their statement, pause to wonder if your teen was already struggling with the historicity of Christianity. Their friend's opinion just may be a way for them to voice what had been niggling in the back of their mind for a while.

Some teenagers communicate by dropping casual statements into the middle of conversations with you, their siblings or friends. When one dad suggested the family pray for their teen's friend, the son said, 'It won't matter. He doesn't believe in God.' That tiny sentence opened a large conversation about how God responds to prayer and who he helps. Little snippets of their responses can help flag up inaccurate threads in our teens' views of God that may need to be pulled out.

Some teenagers communicate by retreating and spacing out during any faith conversations or family prayer. They seem to shut down and their silence makes you worry. Before you try to cajole them into saying more or showing their engagement better, consider whether their behaviour is a clue to the fact that they are struggling with the topic or with what you are requiring from them. If that is the case, maybe they are actually struggling with their view of God.

Some teens may communicate by finding the words to ask questions or to talk about what confuses them; even if it's when you are driving the car, you'll be right there and available to catch those moments and listen for clues about their views of God.

The more we can tune into all the communication our teens are giving us, the more we can begin to identify inaccurate threads of information or experience that they have mistakenly woven into their view of God. Our teens need us to help them pull out those inaccurate threads so they can find a way forward. Course-correcting is a normal part of a teen's lifelong faith journey in learning and knowing God. We do not need to be afraid when their views of God are off, or be worried that it signals the end of the road. We are beautifully positioned to come alongside them and help remove what has gone askew and help them find a more accurate thread to reweave back into their understanding of God.

Broaden their view and experience of God

My mum was an English teacher for most of my teenage years. In fact, she taught at my school. I found it strange to hear my friends and schoolmates talk about my mum, because they had a narrower view of her than I did. They were only with her for a short time every day in class so they mainly experienced the no-nonsense, serious, creative and witty sides of her personality. On the other hand, as her child I got to see many more aspects of her character because I was with her outside of school. I knew her to be relaxed, kind, funny and caring, too. I knew my mum more fully than her students did, because I understood and experienced a greater part of her personality and character.

I'm astonished when I think of all the different aspects of God's nature. Scripture is full of descriptions of him: loving, patient, gracious, kind, generous, helpful, comforting, forgiving, good, faithful, truthful, righteous, jealous, just, holy, mysterious, active, wrathful, all-powerful and all-knowing. The list could go on and on. We need to help our teenagers round out their understanding of God so they can see the depth and breadth of his character and the fullness of who he is.

Often teens' warped ideas of God are narrow views of one or two aspects of his character, so they only see him through a tiny, distorted lens. Because they only have a narrow view of God, they can easily miss out on understanding some of the crucial aspects of his character.

To help our teenager see God accurately, we can give them access to a fuller, broader view of God's character. God can be faithful *and* active at the same time. He can be loving *and* just. He can be strong *and* gentle. He can be all those things and more. As parents we can begin to create experiences through which our teens can better understand the fullness of God's character.

Every family tends to highlight their favourite aspects of God. Some of us want our children to know that God is good, gracious and loving, while others of us want to impress that God is holy, all-powerful and righteous. You may want to think about aspects of God that you as a family seldom talk about. It is helpful for us to realise this tendency of ours so we can be sure to mention the other aspects of God's character once in a while. We don't want to leave gaps in our teen's understanding and experience of the full depth and breadth of the character of God.

We can create windows into our thoughts and experiences as a helpful way of introducing those different aspects of God to our teens. You can do this when you are simply watching David Attenborough's latest documentary series and you mutter, 'I'm constantly amazed at the creativity of God. He could have just made all flowers work the same way, but he didn't. Look at this. Some flowers explode seeds all over the place. Others wait 20 years until they're on fire before they bloom. And those other flowers slyly pretend to be dead to attract flies. God's never-ending creativity is just crazy. He blows my mind.'

Creating windows may mean deliberately introducing your teen to the forgiveness of God by boldly sharing a story of when you messed up. Often, we don't share those stories with our teenagers, but they need to learn how to identify that feeling of knowing they sinned and how God responds to them. You can tell the story while you're walking to a shop by saying, 'Did I ever tell you the time when I stole from my mum's purse and then blamed your uncle?' Tell the story with humour (teens love hearing wayward exploits of their parents) and then create a window into the spiritual implication it had for you. For example:

> Even though eventually Mum figured it out and busted me for it, I still had this weirdly sick feeling in my stomach at night time. I recognise it now as how God nudges me about my sin, but at the time I hadn't felt it enough to know it was God. God works differently with everyone, but for me, it feels like that even now. I just knew I had to sort it with God, but honestly, I was kind

of afraid of what God was going to do. Would he punish me or be angry with me? Would something horrible happen to me if I admitted it to him? I just avoided God for quite a while. Eventually I just ended up outside in the rain on a walk home from school telling God what happened, how awful I felt and how I didn't want to be that person. As I talked, I felt a huge weight come off my chest. I felt light and free for the first time since I did it. Even now, I still like to walk when I tell God my sin and honestly come to him for forgiveness.

You, as a parent, are the expert on your children. As they grow and change, you will be able to spot where your teen may need a broader view of God's character to better understand who God is and how the world works with God in it.

Wade in when they get stuck

Most of the time, our role is to gently shepherd our children to understand God better. But shepherding isn't always about nudging animals in the right direction. Sometimes sheep get stuck or lost. When that happens, a shepherd needs to go find the sheep, pull them out of the bush or hole and place them back on the ground to continue in freedom. Most of the time, our teens will only need that gentle nudging, but there will be times when they seem to be stuck in their faith. When that happens, they need more help from us to gain their freedom again.

We cannot help our children get unstuck by simply telling them the truth as we see it. We cannot argue them into a different way of thinking and we cannot control how they feel. This is when we need to take a step back and have a good look at how they got stuck. We need to see how they've been constructing their view of God and where in that process knots may have formed.

Teens have many strengths, including a laser focus on what they are presently thinking about. Do you remember being a teenager and being fully engaged in an activity or passion? That focus can be help-ful for learning, but it can also cause teens to stumble when it lands on something they can't figure out. They become trapped or stuck.

With faith, teens can be going along just fine, weaving in their threads of truth and experience to their understanding of God, and then one day they stumble across a knot on a thread. Things don't make sense, or a new idea about how God works becomes so significant in their minds that they decide it's all a lie and they've found the thing that unravels all Christianity. They can become obsessed with a question about suffering or comparative religion and begin to focus narrowly on that small knot. Everything else they know about God fades into the background, and they get stuck.

When this happens, they need us to help them unknot what has become tangled in their heart and minds. And, like when we untan-gle Christmas tree lights, we must first step back, take a good look at the problem and find the source of the knot. Then we can help loosen what was stuck and unwind what was tangled.

The key is to position ourselves as assistant un-tanglers, rather than expert problem-solvers. Teens want to be trusted to find their own way out of their problems. If we judgementally say, 'I think you're wrong about God, and I'm going to tell you where you're wrong so you can get over your silly issue and get back to church,' they won't hear us at all. Our job is merely to loosen the knot for them, rather than com-pletely untangle it, so they can finish untangling it on their own.

Observe and reflect
First, we need to bring up the problem of the knot by seeking to under-stand our teen's thought process and by keeping an open approach to their response. For example:

- 'The other day you mentioned that you didn't think God did anything in response to our prayers. Tell me more about that. I'd love to understand more about what led you to that thought.'

- 'Every week you ask to stay home from church. I wonder what makes you feel so strongly about it. Help me understand what it feels like from your perspective.'

- 'You have told me it bugs you that Jesus didn't specifically tell his followers to free all enslaved people. Has that impacted how you feel about God?'

We can then continue to ask open-ended questions that don't seek to teach or correct, but instead help us have a good look at the knot. When we can truly hear our teenagers speak, we can begin to spot where they're stuck. Only then can we help.

Sometimes teens are stuck because they are lacking knowledge of God. If so, we can say, 'You know what really helped me when I was wrestling with this? This Bible verse (or story, sermon or book). It answered my question this way. It might help you, or not. I'm here if you ever want to chat about it.'

One tweenager I worked with had a mum with cancer, and it was making him wobble enormously in his view of God. The father knew his son was struggling with understanding where God was in it all. He sat down with his son and said:

> I don't know why Mum has cancer. I don't think God gave it to her, because that doesn't fit with the loving Father God I know in the Bible and in my life. I'm not sure there is a reason. I think we live in a world that has been broken by sin and evil, and it's not yet fixed and perfect in the way it will be in heaven. Your mum has cancer, and we are all scared and upset about it. What I do know is that God loves me and you and your mum and has promised in the Bible that he will walk with us through everything in our lives. He has promised that he will take away our fear and will fill us with his love. With every tear we cry, he is right there, catching them and storing them up. He is right here, comforting us and helping us. I know that, and I believe that. It

helps me to chat with him about how I feel and to listen to what he says back to me about it. I don't feel alone when I'm with God. In the meantime, the Bible says to keep praying, so we're going to keep doing that.

The father's words helped the son enormously in his faith because, instead of being put in a helpless position, the son was rooted in the truth of who God is, what the Bible says about God and how relationship with God works in a situation like this. The dad loosened the knot where the tween was stuck, and the son knew how to take his next steps with God.

Sometimes our teens are stuck because they are lacking experience with God. If so, we can go about preparing them for future moments with God by creating windows into our own experience with him. One teen girl I know really struggled with the idea of God being with her all the time. Her mother was new to faith, so she was trying to cope with her mother's change. She felt that the idea of God watching her all the time was uncomfortable and intrusive, so she didn't want to engage with anything to do with Christianity. She regularly called God 'a perv' and 'creepy'.

Her mother brought up the topic in order to better understand her daughter's thought process. 'Okay, you keep saying God is creepy,' she said. 'Tell me more. I want to understand.' Eventually she understood what her daughter was struggling with and said, 'I get what you're saying! But, God being with me all the time isn't about God watching me for his own entertainment. That *would* be creepy. I totally understand why you would feel that way.' Then the mother created a window into her own life so her daughter could see what it meant to have God with her all the time:

> You see, the way I think about it is this. God knows all the good bits and the not so good bits about me and loves me totally. He is with me, like sitting right next to me. It's as if I have secret access to my best friend throughout my day. I can talk with him,

and I know he hears me and understands me. He's the best listener ever. He never misunderstands me, and he gives me wisdom when I feel stuck. That's how I think about it.

The girl responded, and they discussed it a little bit more. The mother wasn't sure if it changed her daughter's mind, but over the next few months, the girl softened. She began to engage in church, and she began to chat with God. Eventually, she came all the way into a full relationship with God. She told me that particular conversation with her mother helped her to start thinking differently about God. Her mum loosened the knot, and God and the daughter kept working on unwinding it.

Sometimes our teens are stuck because somehow their assumptions of God have set them up for disappointment.

One teen I knew really struggled when he did not get into the sixth form he wanted. The family had been praying for him to get in, but he didn't. They appealed to the school, and it was rejected. The young man was devastated and angry at God. One quiet evening his dad said, 'I could be wrong, but I get the feeling that you're not just disappointed about the sixth form. I feel this has really impacted how you feel about God. I'm wondering if you might feel disappointed in God, or even angry at him?' The son agreed and told his dad, 'I always thought God loved me and he could do anything. I know *that* school is the best one. I wanted to go there so badly. If God loved me, then why didn't he make a way for me to go to that school?' The dad was silent for a moment and then said, 'Do I love you?' 'Yes,' replied the teen boy. The dad continued. 'Do you doubt that I love you when I don't give you the really good things you want?' 'No, I don't think it has anything to do with your love. It has to do with other things.' The dad nodded. 'God's love doesn't mean that he gives us everything we want. It means he will love us and help us and weave it all together for good. I found that concept helpful for me when I was made redundant, even though we had prayed and prayed. I was still gutted though!' Over the next few weeks, the teen told me how he had been telling

God all his feelings about it, and how he was beginning to feel hopeful that if God said no to this, then he has something better for him. The dad had loosened the knot, and God and the son kept working on unwinding it.

It won't be perfect

Whether we are broadening our teenager's view of God or unknotting where they get stuck, we can help our children see God better and better. None of us have a 100% accurate view of God. Only when we stand before God in the life to come will we fully know him as he really is, and even then we won't be able to comprehend all of him. Until then, we are *all* on a lifelong journey of learning more about God and his character and refining our view of him daily. Our teens are on that journey too. We can walk with them on their path, helping them continually refine their view of God so it can be as accurate as possible, rooting their view fully in scripture and making it alive through experiences with him. As we do so, our teens will begin to see God for who he is and crave a relationship with him.

> None of us have a 100% accurate view of God.

_ 7 _

SURFING THE WAVES

Some of parenting for faith is about proactively equipping our teens for the ups and downs of life with God. We use the tools of creating windows, framing, unwinding wrong views of God, and chat and catch to create space for our teenagers to explore faith at their own pace. We generate these opportunities *for* them. But there are times when the opportunities to help our children's spiritual journeys are generated *by* them.

Teens' lives are like vast oceans filled with unpredictable waves of spiritual interests, emotions, life circumstances and social pressures, all rising up and crashing down one after the other. When these waves happen in their lives, we can gently come alongside our teens and use the tools we've already learned to help them connect with God in new ways.

All we need to do is learn how to surf.

Lessons from surfing 1: not every wave is your wave

When you sit on a beach and look out at the ocean, you notice that the waves are always there. They may be large or small, fast or slow, but they just keep coming. Some waves are better than others, so surfers will paddle out and watch the waves and calculate which ones to catch. If a wave comes that isn't right for them, they will dodge it by riding over or diving under it. Other waves may be perfect, but the surfers aren't in the correct position to catch them. Surfers don't feel under pressure to catch every wave. They jump on the ones they can and let the others pass by. We can do the same.

There will be times when we feel ready and able to jump on a wave in our teen's life and ride alongside them, helping them connect with God in it. Other times, we won't be in the right position or we'll feel it's not a wave we want to surf.

Don't feel bad if you miss out on a wave in your teen's life. Waves are limitless; new ones keep coming all the time. You jump on the ones you can. Don't stress about the ones you can't.

> Jump on the ones you can. Don't stress about the ones you can't.

Lessons from surfing 2: see the waves in your teenager's life

An experienced surfer can see from afar which waves are worth catching and why, based on the size, colour, shape, speed and so on. Once you learn to see the waves in your teen's life, then you can determine the ones worth catching. Here are a few examples of waves to catch.

Interests

Teens' interests often change over time. What is your teen interested in at the moment? It may be books, bands, sport, art, anything. Sometimes a teen may be so obsessed with something that it becomes a significant part of their emotional life, so we may want to catch it.

Spiritual seasons

Sometimes our teen's connection with God comes in waves. They are really into worship music for a few months, and then they go off it. They refuse to attend youth group for half a year, and then suddenly they ask to go every week. They seem to enjoy reading their Bible, and then they hate it. They don't believe in God, and then they seem engaged and interested again. Each spiritual season is an opportunity to surf alongside them and help them find new ways to connect with God.

Curiosity

Teens are curious, and occasionally they may be curious about something that seems random. They may ask intrusive questions about what you are doing in your job or your friendship life. They may hover around the worship team after church or become extremely focused on events happening in the world. When you notice your teen's curiosity bubbling up, catch their wave and feed their curiosity, as appropriate, and help them find God in those things they're curious about.

Anger

What gets them angry? What do they talk the most about? In church, what is the thing that annoys them most? Often you'll find if they vigorously dislike something, that can be a wave to surf as well. Their anger may be directing you to where their passions lie and where they want to be purposeful.

Stories they are interested in

What stories in movies or on TV are they drawn to and why? What characters or personalities do they admire and why? What plotlines interest them, and what challenges do they enjoy watching? The stories our teens are interested in or the characters they identify with often give us insights into their inner life of conflict and growth.

Life circumstances

There will be times when our teens' lives will change and knock them sideways: moving to a new house, a transition into a new school, a family member dying, a personal illness, a crisis of confidence after a bad performance. These changes open opportunities for us to come alongside our teens and help them see God in the midst of it.

Friendships

Teen relationships are rich and varied. At any one time, your teen may be experiencing the joy of a committed friendship, the moral struggles of peer pressure, and ideas of loyalty, confidence and caretaking. These friendships generate many emotional and social waves we can surf using our tools.

Spontaneous faith ideas

Sometimes, your teen will come up with an impulsive idea. They may ask to go to your home group with you or to try a different church. They may discover an app for prayer they like or become interested in joining a team or ministry. Teens are experimenters, and their waves of spontaneity allow them to explore new areas of interest without committing to them. These are beautiful waves to surf with them to help them explore what might be growing in their hearts.

Waves continuously happen and they are well worth watching for, whether you choose to surf each one or not. The more we train ourselves to notice the waves in our teens' lives, the more ready we will be to choose one and come alongside our teen to help them meet God in it.

Lessons from surfing 3: surf the waves in your teenager's life

There is no one right way to jump on board a wave, but we can look at ways we naturally coach our children in life and spot how they can be helpful. Unconsciously, most parents beautifully use the following six ways – six stages – to help their teens get information or values from their heads into their hearts.

I have a friend who loves Leeds United Football Club. His children love Leeds United. Entirely unconsciously, he discipled his children into a love of Leeds United by using these six stages.

1 He **created windows** into what loving this football club meant. He watched the matches on television, wore the T-shirts, defended his team vigorously to others in front of his children, cheered when they won and was gutted when they lost. He knew all the players' details and told his children all about them.

2 He **framed** how the game was played, how the coach was strategising and why he loved this club so much. He framed why he attended the matches, who he went with, where they sat and why. As his children grew into teenagers, they fully participated in the framing with their own opinions and insights.

3 From the time his children were tiny, he **equipped** them to love the team. He covered them in Leeds United kit: onesies, hats, scarves and pennants. He played football with them outside and chose to 'be' a particular player when playing. He bought them posters and taught them all they needed to know to be able to talk about player transfers and offside injustices. As teenagers, they continued to play in the park as a family and made sure everyone knew the latest news on the team.

4 He **created opportunities** for his children to experience the team on TV, and eventually he bought season tickets to take his children with him to the games on a rotation. He wanted them to experience the stadium and the joy and agony of being a fan live in a venue.

5 This father light-heartedly **established boundaries**, swearing off any other colours flying in the house and jokingly ribbing his friends who supported another team. His teenagers occasionally teased him by threatening to support another team, and he teased them back by promising to lock them out of the house if they did.

6 He gave his teenagers fantastic **feedback** by roaring with laughter when they voiced an opinion in line with his own. He swept them up in a hug when they were indignant about a referee call. He listened to their questions carefully and answered them with focus and passion.

Whether it's passing on our love of a football team or how to cope with the opposite sex, these six stages are often present in our parenting and in our natural, everyday lives with our children. We live life in front of them, talk to them about what is happening, equip them to do things for themselves, create opportunities to try things out, establish boundaries for them to live within and chat with them about how their behaviour impacts others.

These six stages are also powerful tools we can use to disciple our teens spiritually. The problem is that with faith, we often miss out on using most of the stages. We default to just using two: creating windows ('See what I do? Okay, now you do it!') and establishing boundaries ('In this family, we go to church!'). If we want our teenagers to fully understand, experience and embrace a walk with God, we need to let our natural coaching happen and consider all six tools as we respond to the waves in our teens' lives.

For instance, when you see a wave rise up, ask yourself, *What does my teen need from me to help them walk with God in this wave?*

- It could be they need you to **create windows**, helping them see where God can be in this season by seeing where God has been in your seasons.

- It could be that they need you to **frame** their situation, helping them see the truth to hang on to or understand where God is in it.

- It could be that they need to be **equipped** to handle the wave they are in. They may need help finding new ways of connecting to God at school or practising practical role-play of how to get out of a party when it's getting uncomfortable.

- It could be that they need you to **create opportunities** for them to try something new or to experience the support they need. They may need you to invite them into spaces they never had access to before or slowly practise a skill that will serve them well now and in the future.

- It could be that they need some **boundaries** to explore their freedom within safely, not being overwhelmed by all the options, but enabled to exercise their choices well, without feeling stressed.

- They may even need some **feedback** to see the impact their choices and character are making on you and the situation. They may need our outside eye of encouragement and observation to help them feel confident in what God is growing in them.

These stages have no start point or end point. Our teens will always be on this journey, and we can continually add to these stages when they need them as they grow and change.

Lessons from surfing 4: work with the currents below the surface

We know that weather can play a part in the shape and frequency of waves crashing on the shore. Surfers and meteorologists can predict changes in the waves based on what is happening in the skies above. But below the water's surface, where they cannot see, are factors that also affect the waves, such as underwater currents and the shape of the ocean floor. At times in our teen's life we may sense that a wave is being affected by deep factors we cannot see, and we may wonder how we can surf a wave we don't quite understand.

Our teenagers often cannot understand what they're feeling, much less why they feel it. When we can genuinely get alongside their hearts and see what is happening underneath their behaviour, then we can understand their feelings, know how to surf their wave and help them connect with God in it.

All teenagers are different. You may have a chatty teenager who shares everything with you, or your teen may barely talk at all. While some parents have the superpower of knowing what is going on with our child by observing them, others of us feel the grief of being powerless and trapped outside our teen's inner life. One way to get our teens talking again is to develop a culture of curious questions.

One way to get our teens talking again is to develop a culture of curious questions.

Teens can smell an agenda a mile away, and they are predisposed to believe that when parents ask questions, it is because we have ulterior motives. They may think we are prying or want information to judge them with. They begin to close us off a little to preserve their independence to make decisions for themselves, but when they fail, they avoid us because of shame and embarrassment that we were right. But what all teens really want is to be understood and supported. If we learn the skill of asking curious questions to understand them better, we can build trust with our teens so they feel our answers help them rather than control them.

Often we approach our teen's heart like a surgeon with an emergency: we want to fix the damage quickly, so we ask questions with the obvious agenda of repairing something right then and there. As a result, some of our teens shut down emotionally before we can make any progress. But suppose we begin having conversations with our teens just to develop a culture of understanding, like a doctor taking a temperature. Then our teens will feel more comfortable with our questions and much less threatened by the process.

This approach goes beyond having good listening skills. It's about working in partnership with God to understand our teen's heart, not just their current problem. It means keeping the conversation going until we can accurately say to our teen, 'Ah, I see. To you, it looks like this and feels like this. I understand now!' Then our teen will be able to say, 'Yes. That's it!' This kind of interaction stirs our compassion: we understand not just what our teen is thinking but also how their heart feels, which we aim to shape.

Good conversations often start with something that makes us ponder. It may be the huge fight we had or a tiny inflexion in our teen's voice at bedtime. God may poke you as you notice a hesitation in a sentence or a reaction that doesn't seem quite right. Be genuinely curious and willing to go down the rabbit hole of questions and answers for the pure sake of gaining understanding. We all long to be understood.

When we genuinely set our hearts on understanding our teen and seeing life through their eyes, we are on a path to building true heart connections with them. It doesn't take much more time than a regular conversation; we just continue it a little longer to see how far it goes. Most conversations take five minutes, and they can be done while in the car, choosing a movie or making dinner. Just be curious and start asking questions. As your child talks, ask open-ended questions or make statements that follow what your child is saying, with no real direction or end goal in mind. Here are a few examples:

- Tell me more about… That sounds interesting!
- What would happen if…?
- Does it feel more like this, or like this? Why or why not?
- What are you afraid might happen?
- How did that make you feel?
- You seem to be feeling… Is that right?
- What happened to make you feel that way? When did it start?
- I've never experienced something like that. Help me understand what it's like.

When you think you understand – when you think you can see the situation from your teen's eyes – summarise it for them in the way you think they would put it. Affirm their emotions while they're at the bottom of the hole. 'I see. It looks like this and feels like this. Wow!' Of course, your teen is feeling what they are feeling. You can see it now!

Respond with empathy

Once we get to the bottom of the issue, we must respond with empathy and compassion, no matter how crazy the problem looks. Too many times, after we have uncovered something in our teenager's hearts, we respond with our emotions: we laugh at the silliness of the fear; we become angry they never told us before; we are shocked at their behaviour or thoughts; or we are visibly relieved. When we allow that to happen, we can lose the influence of the moment because our teenagers then respond to our emotions instead of staying focused on their issues and on what we want to say.

I encourage you to find that place of compassion and understanding within yourself from which you can respond to your teenager's heart in the moment with genuine concern, peace and love.

The next question to consider is: what is the truth that needs to be spoken here? The wisest choice may be to let that conversation settle without resolution. Rather than rush in with an oh-so-wise-and-experienced answer, simply thank them for talking to you about it.

Then you can reaffirm that you respect their independence, and that you are there to help them if they want it. You can say, 'Thanks for sharing that with me. I'm sure you will figure out the right thing to do. I'm here if you ever want to talk about it or need any outside ideas to consider. God's smarter than I am, so he'll have better ideas, but I'm always here too. I'm proud of you.'

You may want to create a window into your life about when you experienced a similar situation, to invite more conversation. For example:

> I once experienced something painful like that. When my friend stopped hanging out with me because of her new boyfriend, I was so hurt. I felt so betrayed and abandoned. I ended up writing a lot in my journal. Pages and pages. It helped me get all the spinning, churning words out of my head. I still write, except now I see my journal as a way of sharing all those churning words with God. How do you cope with that kind of sadness? What works for you?

If your teen isn't sure and wants help, you can surf that wave alongside them, helping them find some next steps. Your teen may not want help, and that's okay too. You are aware of their situation and can watch to see if this wave is one you can surf or just one to watch and be proactive in other ways.

You know your teen, so you will know when are the best times for conversations. Some teens love special face-to-face times with no distractions. Other teens value a more comfortable side-to-side approach that doesn't require the intensity of a face-to-face conversation. Talking while doing something side-by-side often allows teens to open up. It's in the in-between moments where the best small conversations can happen: the five minutes in the car on the way to an activity or the time spent walking to shops or doing dishes.

As a parent, you are perfectly positioned to spot the waves in your teens' lives and discover through conversation the subtle, emotional undercurrents that may be powering them. The more waves you see, the more you can decide which ones are worth surfing and which ones are worth just watching.

Lessons from surfing 5: paddle at the right speed

A surfer has to paddle at the same speed of a wave in order to catch it. If a surfer paddles too slowly, they won't catch the wave's momentum and they'll miss the opportunity; if a surfer gets excited and paddles too fast, they'll remain ahead of the wave and not encounter it at all. Once we see a wave rising in our teenager's life, we can come alongside them and paddle *with* the wave, keeping pace with it, facilitating our teens to connect with God in it and being ready to help with any next steps they may need.

One teenager I know was into creating fantasy worlds. She and her friends would draw maps of imaginary places, create sketches of fanciful creatures and write short stories about their adventures. They were also into fantasy dramas on TV and in movies. Her parents were unsure how they felt about it all, and they wondered how Christianity could 'compete' with the adventure and imagination in those stories. They decided to try to surf their daughter's wave of interest in fantasy.

One day they mentioned that *The Lord of the Rings* had some Christian themes running through it and they asked their daughter for her thoughts on the story. The parents couldn't remember all the characters' names, so the three of them watched the movies together, pausing along the way to discuss the Christian analogies they discovered. Later the parents bought their daughter fantasy books written by Christian authors and they supplied her with the next books in a series she loved. They paid attention to the stories and worlds she created and asked questions about her characters' motivations and conflicts, which opened fascinating conversations about morals, ethics, redemption and forgiveness. Eventually, she began to write stories that integrated Christian analogies. She told me she felt closest to God when she wrote those stories, talked to God about them and thought about his story. Rather than trying to stop their daughter's wave of interest in fantasy, these parents chose to surf it with her instead.

Another teen I know seemed to be going through an intense questioning period in his faith. He was a very analytical young man and had been paying attention to some anti-Christian influencers on social media and at school. His parents were worried that this was the start of their son walking away from his faith. Rather than trying to shut him down, they decided to surf the wave of his curiosity instead. They told their son they wanted to hear more about what he was thinking. He shared with them links to some videos he agreed with and others he wondered about. The parents watched the videos and took their son's interest seriously. Then they rounded up recommendations of good books on apologetics and useful links to online Christian experts in the field they were discussing. They reviewed what they had gathered and brought the best to their son for discussion and debate. They created windows into how they personally wrestled with ideas that required faith leaps and pointed out to their son the facts and solid thinking that led them on their journey to their faith. They contacted people whose brains worked in similar ways as their son's and invited those people over for walks and meals and rigorous faith discussions. Years later, their son told me that what he learned in those years of exploration became foundational to his faith today, even though he didn't see its importance at the time.

In each of these examples, the parents carefully and gently kept pace with their teen's wave. They didn't rush ahead and try to take control of the wave, nor did they drag behind ignoring it. In each example, the parents tried to stay alongside, supporting the wave to continue without getting in the way of the flow.

Lessons from surfing 6: the wave lasts as long as it lasts

Ocean waves are unpredictable in their length and strength. They may last for five seconds, 15 days or 'forever'. Eventually they will end. Some waves break when they're at their largest and collapse without warning; others, after a long and slow run, just peter out along the shore.

The waves in our teenagers' lives will be just as unpredictable. Some of their waves may start out strong but then collapse suddenly. Your daughter may be passionate about mission, but by the time you buy a biography of the missionary she's interested in, she's changed her mind and isn't interested anymore. Other waves may last longer than expected – a favourite video game, a love of a sport, a friendship group that seems to go on forever – so you may have more time to surf the wave alongside them. Because we can't predict the length of each wave, we can choose instead to ride *today's* wave as best we can, following our teen's lead. It may take emotional energy and sacrifice – finding resources, playing games they love, watching a TV show they're deeply into or inviting people into our home – but at some point, the wave will end and we won't have that opportunity anymore.

Since all waves break eventually, be prepared to let them go gracefully. We've all had the experience of trying to continue an activity our child just doesn't want to do anymore. A wave isn't homework they must complete. When you see a wave in their life beginning to peter, bail out before it ends. It's okay. Don't be disappointed or worried that your teen is still struggling or might be backsliding. There's always another wave forming in the distance, and you can catch the next one and accompany your teen on it, finding ways to help them grow closer to God in it.

– 8 –

EMPOWERING PURPOSE

When our teenagers feel purposeful, they feel grounded in the knowledge that they are part of God's plans for today, tomorrow and every day. That knowledge is at the heart of their self-esteem and contentment. We as parents can help our teens develop a life of purpose and learn how to live in it each day.

When we look at the great heroes of faith in the Bible, we can see them as pillars of purpose, living out God's enormous calling. But these heroes didn't know exactly how their lives would unfold, what would happen decades on or how they would die. They just took one day at a time, met the challenges as they came, responded to God's promptings and what they knew to be right, and lived out their purposefulness in God the best they could, knowing they were a part of something bigger than themselves.

When Jesus called his disciples on their life journeys of purpose, mostly it was by simply saying, 'Follow me,' as he did with Matthew (Matthew 9:9); to a few he also said they would be fishers of people (Matthew 4:18–20). When the disciples began their journeys, they didn't know that three years later Jesus would die and then resurrect, nor did they know that he would ascend and they would become leaders of Christ's church. Jesus didn't give them the full, detailed explanation of how their lives would unfold. He just said, 'Follow me,' and they did – step by step, decision by decision, joy by joy, hardship by hardship. And after Jesus' ascension, they continued to seek God's guidance and to follow him even though they had little understanding of what would happen in the years to come. As they followed, they stepped into their purpose for each day.

My prayer for our teenagers is that they would live in relationship with God each day, following him as their lives unfold and impacting others and the world one situation at a time – that this would be their purpose in life.

Many teens today feel the pressure of figuring out where they are heading in life, wanting to know their endpoint before they begin. They feel the weight of choosing GCSE subjects, which set up their A-level choices, which will lead to the possible vocational college or university degree that will define their options for the future. They want to determine their entire life's 'purpose' now. But true purpose isn't found in an endpoint; it is found in following God daily. Often God simply says to us, 'Follow me,' and promises to guide us along the way. As we follow him, our unique path and purpose unfold before us.

> *Many teens today feel the pressure of figuring out where they are heading in life, wanting to know their endpoint before they begin.*

Our teenagers constantly change and adapt, adding skills and growing in their sensitivities and character. Any time we look at them, we see only a snapshot, one moment in their life's journey. Our goal is not to focus on building a path around that single snapshot in time, but to prepare our teens to live their daily purpose in relationship with God and to empower them to follow him wherever he asks them to go.

Jesus summed up how we can live a purposeful life when he answered a scribe's question:

> Jesus replied, 'The most important commandment is this: "Listen, O Israel! The Lord our God is the one and only Lord. And you

must love the Lord your God with all your heart, all your soul, all
your mind, and all your strength.'"
MARK 12:29–31

Jesus also spoke these words to his disciples when he was with them
the evening before he was arrested:

'So now I am giving you a new commandment: Love each other.
Just as I have loved you, you should love each other. Your love
for one another will prove to the world that you are my disciples.'
JOHN 13:34–35

When our teens get stuck on 'What am I supposed to do with my life?'
our answer is twofold:

1 Every day live life with God and love others as you love yourself,
   saying yes to all the things God will prompt you to do each day.

2 Take the next step that God is guiding you to take, trusting that he
   will weave it into your story of purpose.

How do we do this? How do we help our teens live with purpose? We
use all the tools we already know.

Unwind

If our children are to stand firm in their faith and find
purpose in their lives, they need to know the *whole*
gospel story from beginning to end, which includes
God's plans and purposes. The whole gospel story
will give them a framework for understanding God
and the world. God's story is big enough to include all of us. As our
teens mature into adulthood, their understanding of the gospel story
will broaden and deepen, but the story itself, including God's plans
and purposes for them and the world, will *always* remain the same.

So what is the *whole* gospel story, and how does it relate to their reality?

1 **God is love.** He made all things through his vast creative nature and love. He created man and woman so he could love them, and they could respond to him by loving him and those around them. God knows us individually and wants each of us to experience a loving relationship with him.

2 **People walked away from God.** People chose, and keep choosing, to separate themselves from God and his plans and go their own way instead. As a result, the world's systems and societies are broken and not the way God originally designed them to work. We can see all around us the harmful consequences of this: violence, hunger, isolation, pain, mistreatment, insecurity and so on. Sometimes people get confused about the brokenness they see, and blame God for creating it that way or decide he must not exist.

3 **Jesus cleared a way back to closeness with God.** Living in a broken world can be challenging, but we don't need to be afraid or give up hope because God is bigger than all the problems around us. Through Jesus and what he did for us when he died and rose again, we have a way back to living in relationship with God. We can be forgiven for all the clutter that gets into our hearts, and we can begin to love him and other people as he intended.

4 **God is active in the world.** God is constantly at work in the lives of people all around the world. He is helping and rescuing, talking and healing, weaving futures and comforting the broken-hearted. He is doing greater things than we can ever imagine, and he is calling people back to relationship with him. He sometimes invites us to join him in the wonderful things he does.

5 **God gives us his power through his Holy Spirit to join with him in putting love at the centre of everything again.** All that is broken in the world is being changed. If we follow God, he invites us to love

other people and be a part of what he is doing in the world. We can share his story with others, stand up for what is fair, care for the poor and hurting, pray for others, be generous and much more.

6   **One day, God will restore our world to its original design.** One day, when Jesus returns, the whole world will be completely under his authority, and nothing will ever get in the way of our relationship with him or our love for one another.

This is the whole gospel story that we need to teach our teens. It contains a clear sense of God's purpose for us: to know and love God, to live in community, to experience an abundant life in relationship with him, and to work with him as he changes us and the world we live in.

This approach means that our purpose and actions can be seen as part of the whole gospel story. For example, when we talk with our teens about the importance of generosity and sharing, it's because God loves other people as much as he loves us, and they have needs, wants and hurts too. We can partner with God to lift up others and help minister to those in need by giving them what we have, happily and freely. When we see something on the news that horrifies us, we can talk about how to respond with purpose. We can say:

> I'm reminded of that verse in the Bible when Jesus says, 'In this world you will have trouble. But take heart! I have overcome the world' [John 16:33, NIV]. This world is so full of awful trouble. My heart just wants to pray for those people right now. God, thank you that you have overcome this world, and those people need you. Please rescue them and send your angels to protect them and comfort them. Create safe places for them. Help them, God. Show us where we can be a part of what you are doing for them. We are ready and willing, God.'

When our teens know the whole gospel story, they can see that every experience in their life fits into it, and they can be empowered to take their place in it.

Create windows

Create windows into your own journey of being purposeful in your daily life. Let your teens hear why you help with church ministries or why you give someone more of your time. Let them see that even helping people who are struggling in a car park can be part of God's purpose for your day. We often forget to tell these small stories and can find it hard to phrase them without sounding as if we're reporting on a good deed: 'Today I prayed for my friend Devin because he was sad.' But the purpose of telling the story is not to share what *we* did, but what *God* was doing and how he invited us to be a part of it. So we can tell the story like this:

> I was just leaving work, and as I walked past Devin's desk, I just had a gut feeling that I should stop and check on him. Sometimes God does that with me. So, I asked him how he was doing and what he would be up to over the weekend. He took a deep breath and told me his mother was very unwell, and he wasn't sure if she would last the weekend. I just hurt for him. We chatted more about his mum, and he talked about her church. I don't think my colleague has faith, but his mum does. Without really thinking, I told him I would pray for him over the weekend, and he said he would really appreciate it. Then a thought popped into my head to pray with him. I felt it was from God, so I asked if he wanted me to pray for him right then. He said yes, so I said a few sentences asking God to be with him and comfort him and help his mum know peace in her final days. I can't remember what else I said. It wasn't anything fancy. Then I told him I would be thinking of him and gave him my number in case he wanted to talk to someone over the weekend. I love that God prompted me to stop and talk with Devin. I was just going to walk past him. I had no idea he was hurting or was facing something so huge. I love that God knows the hidden hearts of people and lets us be a part of his help for them because then we get to see what he's doing close up.

Our teens also need stories of how God weaves together strands of our lives for his purposes down the road. I remember as a teen being fascinated with how adults ended up in the jobs they were in. The stories were often twisty and unusual. One woman I knew worked high up in the Department of Education, and I was fascinated when she told me her story of how she got there. She started off working with a medical missions group, pioneering new locations where they could help. And then after that she worked in several different churches and was a full-time parent. Somehow every role in her life wove together to prepare her perfectly for her new, influential position in government. That story helped me trust that God will grow in me all the skills I need to accomplish what he will call me to do, and that I could not judge the usefulness of whatever season I was in because I didn't know what God would do with it.

I encourage you to invite people to surround your teen with stories of their journeys with God and how he guided them and wove together the strands of their lives for his purposes.

Frame

Your teens may need you to frame for them how they can be powerful and purposeful just as they are. Teens often feel as if they can't make a difference at school, at home or in the wider world, but they can. Here are a few truths to help them see how.

My presence carries weight

Often teenagers are used to being the 'add-ons' to the more influential people around them, who are usually adults or the natural leaders among their peers. Teens have learned that those people are the ones who decide if they are, or aren't, significant in a particular context. Many teens believe their presence won't make a difference one way or another. When they feel powerless and insignificant, it's easy for them to go along with the crowd.

When we teach our teens to view themselves as having weight, they learn that where they choose to put weight can shift the balance in a crowd and make a huge difference. For instance, their presence at church matters, because just by being there, they bring happiness to others. And when they are in a crowd that starts acting up, their choice of what to do next carries weight and can affect others.

I tell teens that their presence is weighty, and whatever they choose to support, they are responsible for the power they have added to it. They must use that power thoughtfully and purposefully.

My voice impacts others

God's voice to our teens' hearts is filled with love, kindness, encouragement, mercy, wisdom and guidance, and our teens are impacted for good every time God speaks with them. In turn, teens can be purposeful in using their voices – their words – to extend God's love to others. Encouragements and compliments lift people up. Solomon wrote: 'A word fitly spoken is like apples of gold in a setting of silver' (Proverbs 25:11, NRSV). Teens need to learn that their simple, positive words can make a huge impact for good in someone who is having a difficult moment, day or year.

Scripture also says our tongues are like a spark that can start a forest fire (James 3:3–12). Solomon went so far as to say words can bring death or life (Proverbs 18:21). Insults and harsh observations can create long-lasting damage. When teens choose their words carefully to avoid causing harm, they are being purposeful, too. When teens see their friends or others affected by hurtful words or bullying, they can make a difference by coming alongside with encouragement and kindness to help ease the pain.

I am an influential follower

Our teens can sometimes feel they are less important if they are not the leader in a group. I believe that this is because we haven't trained them in the immense power of being a follower. Derek Sivers drew our attention to this phenomenon at a TED conference (see **sivers.org/ff**). He showed a YouTube video taken at a music festival of a lone man dancing wholeheartedly on the side of a hill. Twenty minutes later, a man leapt up and ran to join the dancing man. About 30 seconds after that, a second man leapt up and joined, then five and then 20 and then 80. In three minutes, over 100 people had surrounded this man and were dancing like him and laughing and having a great time. As that song ended, the crowd cheered and lifted the original dancer in the air.

After the video, Derek Sivers posed two questions: 'What made the difference? What created this moment?' In his view, it was the first follower. The first follower turned the wacky guy into a leader. He showed others how to follow and broke down barriers for others to join in. The second follower was also essential, and the subsequent followers added momentum. Still, it took a lot of bravery for the first follower in particular to throw his weight in with the original lone dancer. The first follower's choice changed one man's dance into a movement.

Our teens can be the first follower. Who do they see at church, at school or in the community who is doing something good but needs someone to believe in them, join them and add weight to their voice? What ministry needs their support financially or physically? What lonely teen with a great idea needs someone to come to their meeting? Who is God asking our teens to stand by and be the best follower possible? Rather than thinking, 'Who else will be there?', our teens could ask themselves, 'What would I add if I went?'

I am God's child

When we accepted Christ into our lives, we became children of God. And as children of God, our purpose is to love people as he does.

Sometimes our teens can think, 'Someone else could help that person better. Someone else can solve that problem.' Teens need to know that it's not about being the best; it's about just being willing. Their *willingness* opens all sorts of possibilities for God to use them to affect others and the world. In their willingness, they will find purpose.

When we help our teens understand that they have weight, their voices impact others, they are influential followers and they are children of God, then they can work out their purpose by choosing where to apply themselves.

Chat and catch

Helping our teens find ways of connecting with God also helps them find purpose. There will be times when our teens are burdened by their friends' problems or are stuck in a quandary of their own. They may feel helpless or confused or not know what to do. As they chat with God about their situations, they can gain his wisdom, guidance, courage and peace, and they will feel able and ready to respond to the challenges around them with God's purposes in mind.

Surf the waves

As we parent our teens to know they can be purposeful each day, we can choose to surf some waves in the process. When teens experience a wave of boredom or powerlessness, we can help them learn how to find purpose. We can help them ask questions like 'What is in front of me that needs doing? What am I caring about in this situation? What is God communicating with me to do?'

When our teens are on a wave of purpose and are clear about what they want to do, we can create space for them to do it, be a resource pot for what they need and be their greatest supporter. The most significant ways this will pop up is in the ordinary, everyday ways of supporting friends in pain, helping a neighbour or a small kindness to a family member. Don't be surprised, though, if your teen's personality may also include something formal, like leading a small group at school, starting a charity or business, or joining a church ministry. One is not better than the other, all ways of living purposefully are beautiful.

It is important we surf each wave *with* them rather than try to take it over, and we must remind ourselves that the wave will eventually end. Our teens will make mistakes in working out their purpose in their daily life; it is inevitable. But the joy and confidence they feel as they take responsibility for their personal ministry to others will shape their lives going forward and grow their character and motivation.

Our teenagers are powerful people, called by God to be purposeful each day. He will weave their futures and guide them along the way. If we can help our teens know the joy of purpose, they will find confidence and safety in knowing that whatever comes, they can be a small part of God's great plans for their lives and the world around them.

– 9 –

ENABLING CONFIDENCE

Scripture is full of people who just ooze confidence. Moses and Aaron strolled into Pharaoh's palace to declare God's purpose and said, 'Let my people go!' Jeremiah delivered God's words to kings and rulers with not an eyebrow flicker of doubt. Jesus challenged smug religious leaders and calmly dealt with violent mobs. Young Mary stood boldly under the judgement of her community because she had a deep knowledge of her calling. Paul weathered imprisonment and shipwrecks without fear or worry.

The world has a formula for confidence. It goes like this:

> You are amazing and perfect, just the way you are. People should love and accept you for who you are, and if they don't, that's their problem. Be proud of yourself! Change for no one! Love yourself wholeheartedly! Figure out who you are, then shout it from the rooftops: 'My name is Rachel Turner, and *I am awesome!*'

Some of the Christian community goes along with this formula. We can be told in church:

> God made you perfect and precious. You are unique and wonderful, like a gemstone in his eyes, worthy of so much. To criticise yourself is to criticise your creator. So stand up tall, look in the mirror and say, 'I am perfect just the way I am! I have distinctive talents and spiritual gifts that only I can bring to the world.

I can do all things through Christ who gives me strength. Bring it on! I am special, important, and *I am awesome!*'

We think that if our teens could just believe those statements deep in their hearts, they would be confident. If they could discover who they are and express it well, they would have joy. If only they could live those beliefs, they would be able to weather the storms in the world.

The problem is that the formula doesn't work. Our teenagers are still swayed by the latest trends at school and are still influenced by social media. They are still self-conscious about their voices, their clothes and their bodies. They still get random fears, and they still buckle under performance pressure. We see their confidence being slowly torn away and self-doubt creeping in so we repeat the mantra again and again to them: 'You are perfect just the way you are. You are unique. You are special. You are awesome.' But the inner strength of true long-lasting confidence still seems illusive.

The reason for this is that we have a wrong view of confidence.

Moses didn't successfully lead a nation because he strongly believed in his unique talents. Samuel wasn't confident because he looked in the mirror and truly believed, 'I am special. I am unique. I am perfect just the way I am.' Paul's ability to sing in prison with joy wasn't because he loved expressing his true inner self and had a great singing voice. Mary wasn't bold after hearing that she was to be the mother of the Son of God because she daily reminded herself, 'I am awesome!' So how could they have faced their challenges?

They were able to because their confidence was *in God* and not in themselves. When people in the Bible spoke of confidence, they were almost universally referring to a confidence in God, not a confidence in themselves. As one of the

> When people in the Bible spoke of confidence, they were almost universally referring to a confidence in God.

psalmists wrote, 'For you have been my hope, Sovereign Lord, my confidence since my youth' (Psalm 71:5, NIV; for other examples, see Jeremiah 17:7; 2 Corinthians 3:1–6; Ephesians 3:12).

A healthy core of confidence consists of three beliefs:

- God is awesome and holy, and he loves me totally
- God is daily shaping me to be more like him, and I'm not finished yet
- I am invited to be a small part of God's wonderful plans.

The story of Moses in Exodus 3 gives us a clear example of all three. When Moses approached the burning bush, God told him to take off his sandals because the place on which he was standing was holy ground. And he did. Then God told Moses he had heard the cry of his people in Egypt and he was going to rescue them from enslavement. He commanded Moses to be his spokesman: 'I am sending you to Pharaoh. You must lead my people Israel out of Egypt' (v. 10).

Moses' initial response was to look at himself, his failings and inadequacies, and say to God, 'Who am I to appear before Pharaoh? Who am I to lead the people of Israel out of Egypt?' (v. 11). He knew he wasn't equipped to take on such an assignment. But when Moses expressed his lack of confidence in himself, God didn't rush in and bolster his self-esteem. God simply said, 'I will be with you.' God wanted Moses to know he didn't need to be confident in his own abilities; he just needed to be confident in the God of the universe, who could cover mistakes, change hearts and make up for Moses' weaknesses.

We want our teens to develop a confidence based on the truth that God is the *only* one who can be awesome and holy. We don't have to be. We can't be. And yet, despite our imperfections, God loves us and promises to be with us always and never leave us.

Many teens want to be perfect like the people they see in magazines and movies or the ones in their schools who seem able to achieve all things. Teens want to be perfect *now*, but that is an unrealistic and stressful goal. The truth is: we are all changing and being shaped all the time. Who we are today is different from how we were ten years ago and how we will be in three years.

Think about making a wedding cake. It would be silly to watch the cake being made and then mock the batter for being *only* batter and not the completed cake ready for the big day. After all, it's not finished yet.

Our teens need to know we don't expect them to be perfect or have it all figured out. We know they aren't finished yet. All of us are daily changing and growing as God transforms us to be more like him. And none of us will discover who we fully are until we stand before Jesus at the end – and that will be exciting! For now, we are constantly becoming better and learning more about ourselves and others because God loves us and has put us on that journey of transformation.

Our lives of purpose can take on new meaning when we learn to place our confidence in God and not in ourselves. We can rest in knowing that God chooses us to be part his wonderful plan, not because we are perfect, but because *he* is perfect. And even though God isn't finished shaping us yet, he still asks us to be purposeful in the body of Christ on earth as he weaves us into communities where we can love him and others well and be fruitful in our lives.

So what would teens' confidence look like if they knew a perfect and awesome God loved and valued them just as they are? How much joy would our teens have if they were content with being imperfect and were unimpressed by the world's expectations? What would their days be like if they could walk into school thinking, 'God, what shall we do together today?' instead of 'Please, God, I just want people to like me'?

Here are a few first steps in how we can shift our parenting to build this God-centred core of confidence in our teenagers.

Affirm through relationship, not labels

As parents, we want our children to see themselves positively, so we flood them with encouragements and truths of how we see them. We give them positive labels: you are funny, beautiful, clever, unique. We hope if they believe these statements, they'll be confident in themselves. The problem is that others come along and give them labels too: you are bossy, loud, shy, weird.

Our teens begin to view themselves through the lens of these labels, which can be confusing at times. They can't be beautiful if others think they are ugly. They can't be unique if someone else has the same gifts they do. It's hard for them to decide how to see themselves based by on their labels.

However, their true value is in how *God* sees them, not in how they see themselves. God is the one who loves them and has uniquely made them to fit perfectly in the body of Christ. We can help our teens see how their God-given abilities impact others, how their impact naturally happens when they are just being themselves and how they already have a meaningful place in the body of Christ.

For instance, when people laugh at my jokes or when I can change a serious situation into a light one, I know that God placed in me a capacity to bring joy. When my mum hugs me, invests time in me, smiles at me and asks me endless questions, I know that I am loved and valuable to her.

Try communicating encouragement, love and approval to your children in ways that emphasise your relationship with them and their effect on you, instead of pushing them to accept the label you want them to embrace. For instance, avoid using sentences starting with 'You are' or 'You look', such as 'You are so smart. You are so clever. You are so funny. You are so creative. You look so beautiful.'

Instead, describe how you are affected by who they are or what they do. Here are some examples.

- **I love watching how you…**: 'I love watching how you were so gentle with those babies. I never had that ability with small children like you do, and I admire it. Watching how those crawlers went straight for you when you came in, made me smile. They know that they are safe with you. How wonderful.'

- **I love… about you**: 'I love how your brain works. The way you make connections between different ideas makes me see the world differently, and I so appreciate your wisdom in our conversations.'

- **When we are together, I feel…**: 'I am so happy when we hang out together. It makes me so happy to do chores or watch TV together with you. You just being you makes me smile. I love laughing with you.'

- **When you do… I feel…**: 'When you don't snap back at your brothers, I'm amazed. It shows such self-control and changes how they feel. Your ability to show kindness in the face of unreasonableness makes such a difference to them and me.'

This technique of affirming our teens through relationships rather than labels enables them to not need a list of characteristics – 'I am funny, pretty, wise, etc.' – with which to define themselves. Instead, they simply grow in the confidence that the way they were created, what they have personally been working on and what God has been growing in them are powerful and significant.

Praise what you value

We are imperfect, and slowly we are being shaped by God to be more like Jesus over our lifetime. When we value the character of Christ in our teens, we help them focus their eyes on what makes them more like Jesus.

Often we encourage our children without thinking, maybe in the same way we were praised as children, with words like 'You are beautiful,' 'What a handsome little man,' 'Well done! You won!'

What if, instead of praising according to the world's measuring sticks, we encouraged and praised in accordance with what God has called us to? What would it look like if we deliberately praised our teenagers for the traits we really want to see growing in them? What if we praised our teens not for what we see on the surface but for the deeper values we want to see in their lives?

When we look in scripture, we can discover many qualities in Jesus that we want to see and encourage in our teens. For instance:

- Love of learning
- Ability to see opportunity in failure and to bounce back easily
- Curiosity
- Deep compassion
- Love
- Joy
- Peace
- Patience
- Kindness
- Mercy
- Grace
- Humility
- Goodness
- Gentleness
- Faithfulness
- Self-control
- Courage
- Sacrifice
- Generosity

- Love of team
- Ability to value others' contributions
- Wisdom
- Boldness
- Justice
- Perseverance
- Ability to problem-solve
- Ability to be a good friend
- Honesty

Note that this is not a gendered list. It's a list of character traits God has called us all to develop, no matter what our gender. It is important that we praise both our young men and young women for their kindness and self-control, as well as their bravery and sacrifice. These character traits reflect Christ, and we are each called to be like him.

When we stop praising superficial values, like cleverness, beauty or strength, and start praising the biblical character traits and truths we see in our teenagers, those traits will develop and blossom.

Value imperfect progress

When we place our core confidence in God, we begin to feel comfortable in the fact that we are not finished growing yet and that God *still* invites us to be a small part of his great plans everyday, just as we are. We realise that who we are today isn't who we will be tomorrow, because God is still shaping us and we are an active part of that process. Labels don't fit us because they are static, and we are constantly changing.

To make imperfect progress a part of our teenager's world view, we need to create a culture in our homes where changing, learning and improving are regularly celebrated, discussed and expected. It starts with us creating windows about our own current progress in transformation. Talk about what you are learning at school or work. Share stories of how you are changing in response to scripture or circumstances. Share what you and God have been talking about. Apologise when you need to, and discuss what it's like to be on your own journey of transformation.

Talk about labels you believed about yourself, and how at times you placed your confidence in them, instead of in God. Have conversations about characters in movies and on television who constantly talk about 'being themselves'. Invite your teen into a conversation about what that phrase means and why the character would say it.

People in the Bible have great journeys with God in which they grow and change. Discuss the changes you see in Jesus' disciples and in people such as Esther and Joseph, and notice how God continued to develop them throughout their lives.

Valuing imperfect progress even extends to our discipline. Teens become frustrated when they feel they have made progress in something but we don't appreciate it and only seem to focus on the shortcomings that still remain. They can be disheartened when they feel we expect perfection they can't deliver on. If we don't acknowledge their progress, they feel unheard and unappreciated.

> Valuing imperfect progress even extends to our discipline.

One teen I talked with had made what she thought was a huge effort to tidy her room before her dad asked her to. She expected her father to notice her effort and responsibility, but instead he came in and pointed out where she had fallen short. After our session on valuing imperfect progress, the girl's parents began to look out for when she was trying to be proactive and progressing in responsibility. Her dad began to say, 'Thank you so much for remembering to tidy your room. That builds my trust in your ability to manage yourself. It looks great! Could you please empty your bin, too, before you watch TV?' That little change in language made a massive difference in their daughter's motivation and confidence because she felt her efforts were being noticed and appreciated.

Whether it's cleaning a room, managing anxiety patterns or persevering with communicating with you, we can notice and appreciate all the progress our teens are making. When we help them see the fruit of their progress, we can celebrate their growth with them while not giving up on our ideal for them. This can be balm to a teenager's soul. It says to them, 'I see you and I appreciate you. And we can look at the rest, but you've made progress.'

Teenagers see that we, too, are fallible humans who aren't perfect. Teens can feel satisfaction in noticing and pointing out our imperfections. While this can be a painful experience for us, it also gives us a wonderful opportunity to show them that seeing someone's imperfection isn't a 'gotcha' moment. If we begin to create strategic windows into our own imperfect progress – how we feel when we get things wrong, what we do when we fail, who God is in all of it and how we connect with him – we help our teens learn and understand that life is not about any of us being perfect. Instead, it's about all of us growing and changing and encouraging each other in the progress we're making.

Some families have developed ways to talk about imperfect progress which may be helpful to you:

- 'I don't expect perfection; I expect progress.'
- 'I don't need you to be perfect because none of us will ever be perfect, but I know 100% that you can progress a little bit at a time. If I don't notice, please tell me so I can appreciate it.'
- 'I'm still growing, and you're still growing, and there's always going to be something to get better at.'
- 'No one's perfect on the outside, and no one's perfect on the inside. And so you can't expect your friend to be perfect. We're all imperfect people who are being transformed daily to be more like Jesus, and we're not finished yet. So when you choose

a friend or partner, it's important to look for people who are committed to growing and changing to be like our ultimate friend and partner – Jesus.'

Our teen's core of confidence isn't about them thinking they are perfect; rather, it's about trusting that, although they are still growing and changing, God loves them just as they are and he has created them for a relationship with them and to have a significant impact on the people around them. That's the biblical core of confidence.

* * *

For more tools on walking with our teens through the modern world of media, peer pressure, comparison, beauty standards, envy and failure, go to **parentingforfaith.org/topics/teenagers**

– 10 –

CONNECTING OUR TEENS INTO CHURCH

Getting our teenagers to church and hoping that they love it can occupy a large part of our brain space. The subject seems full of pitfalls. If we force them to come to church, will they rebel? If we do not make them come at all, will they ever understand the importance of church? It seems whichever way we turn is wrong, and it feels stressful. And rightly so. A recent survey revealed that 70% of 18–22-year-olds leave the church when they leave home, some temporarily, some for good. This doesn't mean that 70% are losing their faith; rather, they are losing the habit of connecting with a church family. If we want our teenagers to continue to see church as a part of their future life, we need to help them find their place in it.

When we value something, we want our children to value it too. We want our children to see and love the church, not just tolerate it. We want our children to truly engage and connect with our church, because it is a family of God who will love and encourage them. It is a community who will support and inspire them to know and love God and help them grow in connection with him. God designed it to be a deep and powerful blessing for us all, and we want our teens to experience that.

So how can we help our teens grow in their love of the church and learn how to engage with it to the fullest?

Experiencing the British Museum

One of my favourite places in the world is the British Museum in London. The building itself is gorgeous, especially the great court with its gleaming white walls and glass ceiling. I love just sitting there, watching people mill around and hearing the sound of different languages. I love the murmurings in the central library room and the smell of dry, old books stacked up to the heights. I love walking through rooms full of history, seeing ancient everyday artefacts and works of artistic creativity. I can't help but smile as I walk past people calling each other over to point out what they've just discovered or to share what they've just learned. I am thrilled when a docent gives a demonstration and invites me to touch objects from the past: a coin from China in 342BC or a figurine from ancient Mesopotamia. There is so much to love about this museum.

One time I was in the British Museum taking a break between meetings, and a school group arrived for a short trip to see Egyptian artefacts. The teachers and volunteer parents had the children in lines and conducted them with lightning speed through the gorgeous atrium. When several children slowed down to gasp at the beautiful space, a parent intervened with a quick, 'Don't stop to stare. Keep moving!' and then shuffled them back to their place in line. It wasn't long before another two children spotted some African figurines through a side door and with overwhelming joy started running towards them, only to be caught by another observant parent who directed them back to the group.

I watched the students as they entered the Egyptian rooms and were dispersed to explore the exhibits and complete their tasks. Some loved the place immediately, but others became bored and restless and struggled to stay focused. I heard some, who moments ago had been swept away by the grand entrance or the African figurines, now commenting how boring the museum was.

I was so frustrated. The museum is more than just a few statues to see – it's also the environment, the sensory experience, the history, the creativity and the community of learning. It's a place where everyone can find something intriguing and relevant to their current interests or their past, and everyone can be fascinated and challenged by being exposed to something different. And yet, for most of these children on this specific trip, they missed all that. Their experience was completely focused on the task at hand: the time-limited group activity assigned to them. They visited the British Museum, but they didn't truly experience it.

Our teenagers' experience of church can often be similar to this. Life gets busy, and our concept of 'helping our teens engage with church' easily slips into 'helping our teens survive a service without too much eye rolling' or 'dragging our teens to the youth group or Sunday service'. We can accidentally become so focused on having them complete the task at hand that they miss the endless beauty and opportunities of the wider church experience.

We are in the beautiful position of helping our teens navigate through the different aspects of church without leading them around like students. We can help them learn to engage with the church in their own way, pursue their own varied interests in their own time and cherish the aspects of church they choose to explore.

To fully explore the wonder of the church would require a whole book in itself. For our purposes, let's focus on just a few significant aspects. Feel free to choose others or add your own to this list. The point is that our teens need to experience and learn how to engage with many aspects of church. Once we identify ones we want to focus on, we can begin to help our teens engage with them proactively. I would suggest these aspects as a start:

- **Drawing near to God** (Hebrews 10:19–24; Acts 2): The church is a place to wholeheartedly encounter God through worship, preaching, kids' groups and prayer times. We want our teenagers to meet with God through the community and activities of the people in our church.

- **Radically loving others** (John 13:34–35; Acts 2): The church is a place to radically love and encourage others, and to receive that love and encouragement in return. We want our teenagers to sacrificially and joyfully put down their lives for each other, to be full of compassion and love and to draw alongside other people on their journey. We want them to receive all that from the community as well.

- **Spurring each other into action** (Hebrews 10:23–25; Mark 16:15–20; Acts 11:19–30): The church exists in part to enable Christians to challenge and support each other, to wrestle with scripture together and share their tough questions, and to be part of a group that encourages and equips each other to live a life that honours God and what he has called each one of us to do.

- **Giving each part a purpose** (1 Corinthians 12:12—13:13; Ephesians 4:11–16): The church is a place where every person is a purposeful part of the body of Christ and is needed by the whole church, and where we can all value the contributions of others. We want our teenagers to see that they are valuable, unique and useful in the greater calling that God has for his church.

- **Pursuing the Spirit** (Galatians 5:16–26; Acts 2): The church is a place to pursue and experience the work of the Spirit, both in the internal transformation of becoming more like Jesus and in participating in his active work in the world.

When we begin to reflect on these aspects of church, we can then assess how our teenagers are engaging with them in the fullness of church, and we can create new ways to enable our children to experience them. For us to do so, we need to grow in our own confidence of proactively helping our children grasp these concepts.

Using the six-stage circle to disciple our children

The joy of already knowing the aspects of the church we value is that we will always be able to find a place for our children to explore spiritually. If our teenagers are struggling with the service, we don't need to double down on forcing them to like it. They may simply be ready to explore a different aspect of church, and we can help them take that next step in their exploration. Maybe we have been pushing them to draw near to God in the service, but their next step may be to dig into loving others and feeling loved by them. Or if they are getting bored with the preaching, then it may be time to enable them to find their own purpose within the church community.

If our teenagers are struggling with the service, we don't need to double down on forcing them to like it.

As we disciple our children through their new explorations, we can use all the six stages that we saw in chapter 7 – that is, create windows, frame, equip, create opportunities, establish boundaries and give feedback. All six stages flow together in a circle with no starting point or end point, as shown in the diagram on the following page.

Let's look at how to use this six-stage circle to help our teenagers explore two specific aspects of the church: drawing near to God during sung worshp, and spurring each other into action. Remember, you are the experts in your teens, so only you know how these six stages will work best with them. The following are merely examples to illustrate the possibilities.

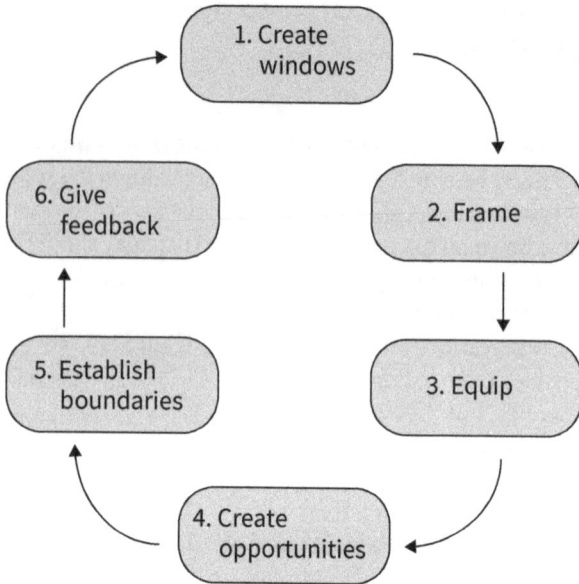

Using the six-stage circle: drawing near to God during sung worship

There are many ways we draw near to God at church: through relationships, prayer and meditation, being taught by sermons and hearing testimonies, listening and reading scripture, and participating in worship. Let's take a moment to discuss sung worship – the time during a service or small group when we sing to God with music. If your churchmanship doesn't use sung worship, consider the six-stage circle with a different central aspect of your corporate encounter with God: for example, the long silences or the reading of the Bible.

1 **Create windows:** One of the most powerful things we can do for our teenagers is to genuinely worship in front of them, whatever that looks like for us. Whether you raise your hands, sing loudly

or stay silent, create a window for them to see you drawing near to God during worship time. When they see you, and others they know, authentically connecting with God through music, they see that they can connect with God through music too.

2 **Frame:** Connecting with God during singing can be a challenging concept for teenagers to grasp. During the service, or on a walk mid-week, you might want to say, 'How are you finding the music part of the service? It's supposed to be a time of drawing near to God and him drawing near to us. Does it feel like that for you? Why or why not?' You can explain what it is like for you and how worship works. Here are some aspects of worship I've found myself explaining to youth:

'Sometimes the words allow my heart to express something I haven't thought of saying to God. The words also give me a truth that I need to be reminded of. Sometimes I sing the words because I want to mean them. Other times I stay silent and listen with my eyes closed because I want the truth to sink into my heart.'

'You can sing as quietly or as loudly as you want. No one is listening. Even if you don't know the tune, it's okay.' (Teen boys in particular sometimes struggle to sing during the musical worship. Their vocal changes make it hard for them to feel comfortable guessing what sound their voice will make. They may need some specific permission to find what works best for them.)

'The point of sung worship is to engage with God. Some of us struggle to read the words fast enough to keep up with the songs, and so I know people who prefer to sing only the lines they like when they are repeated. I also know people who like hearing other people sing the words so they can nod along. What is important to me is that you are connecting with God, not that you are singing.'

3 **Equip:** Our teens may need help engaging in the worship. If they don't know all the words to a song, play it around the house. Sometimes songs have very Christian phrases they might not understand, so you may need to quickly lean over and whisper what 'Yahweh' or 'The lion and the lamb' means. If you don't know, you can lean over and say, 'I don't know what that means, so let's figure it out later. I'll just hum along for this one.' Our teens may also need to be equipped to proactively decide what type of worship works for them. One teenager told me that he loves worshipping at home alone but hates worshipping at church with his family in the front row because he feels as if everyone is watching him. He said his parents told him he could feel free to move to whatever spot works best for him. They said that having a place to comfortably worship was more important than sitting together as a family. So now, when the worship happens, he just slips out and sits on the floor behind the pews to worship without being seen. That has significantly changed the way he feels about worship in church.

4 **Create opportunities:** The more opportunities teenagers have to find their own comfortableness in worship, the more they will value it. We can help our teenagers explore drawing near to God by enabling them to go on their journey of how to connect with God at church. It could be that a contemporary evening service or one with a quiet meditative style may fit your teen better. Let them try a different service, and if they don't continue with it, that's okay. What they gain from the experience will still be valuable and can open conversations. When your teen says, 'I just don't like the music here,' it doesn't allow for much growth. But if they can say, 'I like this music better and I feel more connected to God when I hear it,' you can then ask questions: 'Why? What is the difference? How did your approach change in connecting with God? Can you have that same experience at home? Is worship dependent on the style of music? Why or why not? How can I help you connect with

God?' Your teen may find new ways to connect with God in your worship service, or they may find a new worshipping community that helps them connect with God more. The point is to go on the journey with them and equip them to find a place where they can draw near to God with others.

5   **Establish boundaries:** Feel free to create boundaries. You can say, 'This is our time to draw near to God, and because of that I don't want you to play on your phone or tablet,' or, 'This is the time we draw near to God. How do you want to do it?' This is an important aspect of empowering our teens to find their own paths. Rather than dictating what their behaviour should be, we can say to them, 'You have vast freedom within this boundary.' One young teen I knew had this freedom within his parents' boundaries and landed on just reading the words and not singing. He said that listening to people sing words about God and being able to read them made him feel wrapped with a blanket of faith that made him feel safe. He said that when his parents made him sing, he was so busy reading and trying to figure out the melody that he never knew what the words were. Once his parents gave him the freedom to find his own way of connecting, he said that he could finally connect with God through the words.

6   **Give feedback:** Spend time after church talking with your teens about their experience of drawing near to God in the worship and why it was like that. You can talk about what got in the way of them worshipping or what made the experience particularly special. Whether it's in worship, prayer or engaging with scripture, by helping our children explore the value of drawing near to God during services and midweek groups, we can empower them to find him near in every context.

Using the six-stage circle: spurring each other into action

1 **Create windows:** To get our teens to experience the wonderful challenge and encouragement of being part of the church, we can begin by creating windows into what it means to spur on others in the faith and to have others spur us on in our own journey. Let your teenager see you listening to other people's sermons and to other members' wisdom and insights about God and scripture. Talk about how an experience with God or scripture changed you, or how a friend challenged you theologically or personally.

2 **Frame:** Frame for your teen how one part of being in church is being vulnerable enough to share what we are feeling and thinking, and being open to receiving the encouragement and challenges of the community around us. When someone in your congregation encourages you in person or through email, share it with your family and tell them how their words strengthened or excited you to continue in your efforts.

3 **Equip:** As teens grow, they learn how to spur people on – how to encourage without forcing and how to challenge without crushing. Sometimes teens need to practise this skill in their families. Take a few minutes to describe how 'spurring each other on' works: we can remind people of forgotten truth, speak courage when people have lost hope or cheer people on when they get tired and want to give up. When you notice your teens doing this, let them know how it impacted you: 'What a great encouragement. I feel like I can do this now,' or, 'I love how when your brother thought he couldn't do his homework, you reminded him of times when he persevered and succeeded. Thank you for encouraging him.'

4 **Create opportunities:** Life is full of opportunities to invite our teens to spur us and others on to good works and faith. When you are feeling discouraged, feel free to share a bit with your teenager and tell them you need some spurring on. You can say, 'I need a

new perspective, and I value your insight and encouragement. What good things am I missing out on seeing?' or 'Your sister had a rough day, and she really looks up to you. Can you find a way to encourage her today?' When we create opportunities for our teens to encourage us and spur us on, we need to make sure we give feedback well so they can see the change. We can also begin to look around as a family and come up with plans to spur others on. Who is doing a project that needs encouragement and help? What could we do to jump on board and strengthen and encourage others in what God has called them to do within the church community?

5 **Establish boundaries:** Boundaries aren't just restrictions, but they are also standards to hold ourselves to. We need to use our words and actions to encourage and motivate each other, not tear each other down. And so we must encourage people when they step out and participate in the church community. Create a culture of encouraging the preacher of the day or thanking someone for their ministry by telling a story of how they impacted you. We can train our teens how to use their voices not just to say thank you, but to encourage others more sincerely.

6 **Give feedback:** Help your teens see the impact of their acts of spurring others on. Show them how things could not have been done without them, how their words blessed people and how their actions enabled others' callings. Show them the powerful effect people can have in the world when they spur each other on.

Remember, no matter what your teenagers are feeling about church, they can always take the next step into a new area of exploration within the church. If drawing near to God seems to be causing a struggle, then suggest they focus on something else. They may be ready to just embrace the community of church and find significance in that. Or they may be ready to wrestle with the sharpening aspects of learning and being part of a challenging team. Remind yourself of all the different aspects of church you treasure, and help them find their next step.

Should I make my teenager go to church?

We often look for a yes-or-no answer to this question, but I don't think it is as simple as that. I think the question needs to change from 'Should I make my teenager go to church?' into a much more helpful 'What aspects of church do I think are important for my teen to engage with in this season and how can I facilitate that?'

When we pivot from a simple yes or no, it opens opportunities to find the right path for our teens. Only you know your teen well enough to know what aspect of church is vital for them in this particular season.

One teenager I worked with was passionate about rugby and, unfortunately, his matches typically were played on a Sunday morning. His mum was agonising over whether to take him out of rugby so he could continue coming to church. She decided to give him the opportunity to choose how he engaged with church. She told him that she felt it was important he was connected into church for relationships with people who loved God and loved him, so he could connect with God and serve others. But she didn't mind how he found a way to do that within the wider opportunity of church. She told him to let her know how he would make that happen.

So, he started to look at midweek groups and youth groups. He tried out the evening service and an adult home group. Eventually, he decided he would attend the 8.00 am Book of Common Prayer service on Sundays and serve within the service too. His mum was sceptical. Her son had never shown an interest in liturgy or hymns, but she was willing to let him take the lead as long as he found people who loved God and loved him, could connect with God and serve others.

He absolutely loved it. He adored the peace and space that the quieter service provided. He was the only person at the service under the age of 70, so he was adored by a bunch of older adults who adopted him. They showered him with love, attention and cakes, and some even came along to watch him play rugby after the service. He served as a welcomer on the team, served as a Bible reader and occasionally shared a sermon with another preacher.

Another teen I knew was massively struggling with connecting to God and was retreating more and more into himself at church, growing hostile and resentful. His dad felt his son needed to participate in some activity where he could feel valued and a part of the church community. So, he told his son that he wanted him to get involved in the church community in a way that made him happy, but it was up to him to decide how. The teenager liked hanging out with small kids, so he asked if I needed any help in the children's ministry. I put him for a trial in the 3–4-year-olds' room on a Sunday, and he instantly became like a rock star to them. He was brilliant with the children, and they loved him. He was hooked.

Before each service, the children's ministry team would meet to discuss the new session and pray together, and they included the teen boy in their meetings. They invested in him and made him feel valued, seen and loved. In the sessions, the team read the Bible, prayed with the kids and played games with them. The teen spent the next four years with those children every week, moving up the age groups with them until he went to uni, where he continued to serve in children's ministry in a local church. This teen boy drew near to God better by serving than passively listening in the service.

One parent approached me and said her daughter was struggling with services, so she was giving her daughter permission to stop going to church altogether as long as she invested in a small community of people. The daughter joined the adult home group meeting in her home and was able to slowly be loved, heard and valued by them week after week. They prayed for her exams, interceded over boyfriend trouble and were invested in her as a person. She blossomed within that small community, helping with practical needs and eventually doing some of the teaching in the group every once in a while. Her faith grew steadily, and she experienced the blessing of church through their home group.

Only you will know what season of church exploration may be next for your teenager. Remind yourself of all the reasons you love the church, and help your teens discover them all. Don't worry if they are struggling with one aspect of the church. Help them explore others. Within the ones we've already mentioned – drawing near to God, radically loving others, spurring each other into action, giving each part a purpose and pursuing the Spirit – our teenagers have plenty of space to grow and connect with the church.

* * *

For more on parenting teens for a life of faith, follow Parenting for Faith on social media (see the facing page for how) and also take a look at **parentingforfaith.org/topics/teenagers**

Stay connected!

Do you hope to raise children and teens who stay connected to God throughout their life's journey? The good news is you can! We believe God has placed you in the perfect position to do just that. We'd love you to be part of our supportive community of parents, extended family members, carers and church leaders, so you can find exactly the help and encouragement you're looking for, 24/7.

Find us on social media

facebook.com/parentingforfaithBRF

twitter.com/godconnected

instagram.com/parentingforfaithbrf

YouTube youtube.com/brfcharity

The Parenting for Faith podcast

Don't miss our regular Parenting for Faith podcast covering up-to-the-minute issues, questions from parents like you, special guests and interviews. Find it wherever you normally listen to podcasts or go to **parentingforfaith.org/podcast.**

Reflections and suggestions online

Maybe you're wondering how to help your kids cope with challenges at school or what to do about Halloween. Perhaps your children feel God can't love them because of what they're going through or you're trying to help them develop gratitude. You might be struggling to know how to help a child with additional needs connect with God.

Whatever your concern, you can be sure someone has been there before you. We've commissioned a collection of well over 300 topics, from the Parenting for Faith team and from parents just like you, writing and speaking from their own experience.

Find just what you need, just when you need it, in the searchable library at **parentingforfaith.org/topics**.

The Parenting for Faith course

Doing the course was life-changing in terms of my parenting, and it was amazing as a pastor to see significant changes happening in the lives of the participants. We can't wait to run it again!
Course participant

If you're looking to transform how you do faith in the home, why not think about running our video-based course in your church, among your friends or even by yourself or with a family member? People regularly tell us it's been a 'game changer', bringing renewal not just to families but to whole churches.

The Parenting for Faith course is available to download or live-stream from any device, with free handbooks and promotional materials for groups. For those who prefer DVDs and printed handbooks, these are available to buy from BRF.

Find out more at **parentingforfaith.org/course**.

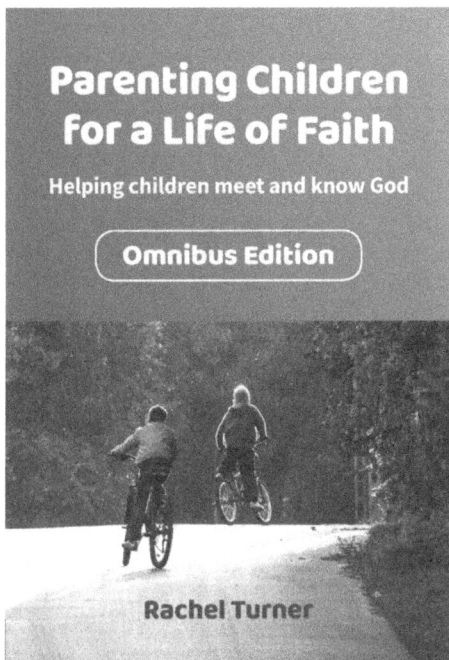

Parenting Children for a Life of Faith

Helping children meet and know God

Omnibus Edition

Rachel Turner

Equipping parents to raise God-connected children and teens. Collecting all the wisdom of titles previously published as *Parenting Children for a Life of Faith*, *Parenting Children for a Life of Purpose* and *Parenting Children for a Life of Confidence*, this book provides inspiration and wisdom for nurturing children into the reality of God's presence and love, equipping them to access him themselves and encouraging them to grow in a two-way relationship with him that will last a lifetime.

Parenting Children for a Life of Faith – Omnibus Edition
Helping children meet and know God
Rachel Turner
978 0 85746 694 5 £12.99

brfonline.org.uk

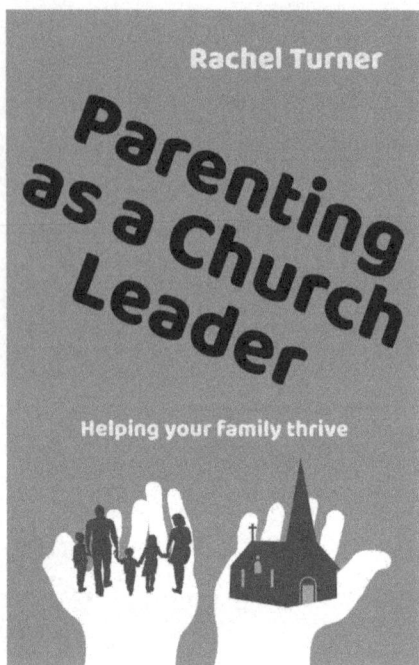

Rachel Turner

Parenting as a Church Leader

Helping your family thrive

When spiritual leadership is the day job, how does it affect family dynamics? How do we spiritually parent our children while also needing to lead the church? How do we balance the many hats we wear? How do we live in a goldfish bowl and yet enable our children to flourish? How do we parent for faith without giving in to the pressure to perform for our congregations? Drawing on extensive research, this book explores the issues and builds a set of simple tools and approaches to help leaders and their families to flourish together.

Parenting as a Church Leader
Helping your family thrive
Rachel Turner
978 0 85746 937 3 £9.99

brfonline.org.uk

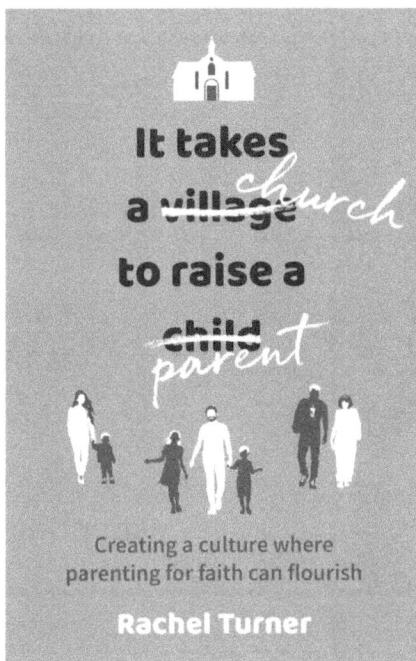

It takes
church
a ~~village~~
to raise a
~~child~~
parent

Creating a culture where
parenting for faith can flourish

Rachel Turner

Parents are the primary disciplers of their children, but we as a church are called to be their community who supports them as a family, equips them to succeed, and cheers them on the path of parenting for faith. This book will help children's, youth and senior leaders to learn how to position themselves for maximum impact, develop foundational values and practices to operate out of, and establish practical steps to shape a culture where parenting for faith can flourish.

It Takes a Church to Raise a Parent
Creating a culture where parenting for faith can flourish
Rachel Turner
978 0 85746 625 9 £8.99

brfonline.org.uk

BRF

Enabling all ages to grow in faith

Anna Chaplaincy
Living Faith
Messy Church
Parenting for Faith

BRF is a Christian charity that resources individuals and churches. Our vision is to enable people of all ages to grow in faith and understanding of the Bible and to see more people equipped to exercise their gifts in leadership and ministry.

To find out more about our work, visit

brf.org.uk